Oneness of All Life

By Marjorie H. Russell

Unity Books
Unity Village, Missouri 64065

Cover photographs: sky, Katherine Weedman; dragonfly, berries, autumn leaves, Keith McKinney; ocean, Marjorie Russell; wheat, staff photo.

Inside art: Marjorie Russell.

Contents

Harmony

I stand today beside the sea,
And hear the ocean roll,
And all is one vast harmony,
An anthem of the soul.

The rocks, the seaweed, and the sand,
The little sky-blue cove,
The sunlight falling on my hand,
Are all a song of love!

What poet but Almighty God
Could breathe this world to birth,
Could sing green verses into sod,
And rhyme the roots of earth?

What poet but immortal Faith
Could make a man like me,
Could live in him and give him breath,
And say unto him: "Be!"

What poet but eternal Truth
Could hide Himself so well—
Be winter wisdom, April youth,
Be flesh and ocean shell,

Be lowly dust, be star and tree,
Be gull that soars above,
And blend and be the harmony?
None but the highest Love!

By Elizabeth Landeweer

Rhodora
M. Russell

Life Together

Throughout the centuries Christians have found God through nature. Saint John of the Cross, Saint Hubert, Saint Francis, and others caught the peaceful essence of the beloved within, beneath, around all living creatures. How, then, can we seekers of life eternal escape the thrill that awaits us from pleasant perusals of nature's quiet woodlands, streams, and arching skies?

Wherever one looks, one discovers a friendly God. All organisms, however small, are not alone. The whole living Earth is one composite togetherness. Within and yet behind each invisible atom reposes the life, order, love, and intelligence of Spirit, transmitted from the absolute into a condition that appears as dense matter. Behind each waterfall, every ripple in the sea, each furrow of brown earth, within the throbbing breast of every singing bird and each brilliant flower is the presence of the Infinite, carrying out its plan and purpose.

Although there are many who believe in a competitive, self-survival, self-sufficient slant on nature, there are some who believe that nothing exists in or of itself. There is an interrelatedness existing between all things that leads us to conclude that life does not evolve because of competition but because of cooperation.

Sir James Jeans, in his book, "The Mysterious Universe," propounds that the universe appears to be a great complex thought, as the mind of the Great Architect thinks His thoughts into being. We can also agree that he has a credible postulate in that every bit of the universe seems to know what every other bit is doing, and acts accordingly. It is concerned neither with distance nor variation of purpose. It is only being what it is supposed to be, and doing, to the height of its ability, what it is supposed to do in cooperation with every other living thing.

Before our era, man peered suspiciously at nature with dim eyesight and dulled hearing. He appeared to be alone on the outside of life's mysteries. As he probed to "get in," feverishly trying to comprehend the miracles around him, he eventually came full circle to discover those same outer miracles were an intrinsic part of his own being.

As each part of the life of God beats in harmony, eternity dawns fairer and more beautiful upon our conscious awareness. Now we know that the wealth of God surrounds us and weaves a web of amber, green, crimson, blue, and violet rays that spell one enchanting word: oneness. Indeed, it is impossible to say where one form of life leaves off and another begins, because within the outline of each resides a Creator that will not be confined. It focuses into expression and then expands into infinity.

It has been said that we must learn to defend ourselves against the tyranny of increasing mass media, but few have suggested how this is to be done. Today we are witnessing a sharp increase of interest by the scientific world in natural phenomena, which is perhaps part of our defense mechanism for self-survival but also partly due to our realizing the necessity to attain peace of mind, which comes by conscious union with the order of creation.

Whenever we indulge in anger, hate, resentment, fear, or false judgment, we isolate ourselves from every living thing. Such negative thoughts and attitudes defy nature and the peace and power that run the universe. Isolation is not natural.

The dynamics of natural life involve complex

interaction and oneness of will that is startling. Whereas human beings often work in counteraction to nature and try to maneuver specific lifestyles, nature left to itself will settle into a harmonious pattern, secure and productive.

Whether this life action takes place through a bird's rendering its sweet melodies of joy and helping to maintain balance as a predator or through algae and fungi living on the same rock, the fungi getting food from the algae and the algae getting water from the fungi, or through a bee visiting over four thousand flowers to make a tablespoonful of honey, simultaneously pollinating the species to increase production, it is still love providing for itself through a harmonious interaction as all forms of life move forward in mutual reciprocity.

It was Johannes Kepler, a poor, gentle, sickly assistant to the German scientist Tycho, who in the early 1600s brought to the race many new awarenesses, among which was the possibility of the harmony of the spheres. From mathematical calculations and observations he transposed the relative velocities of the different planets into what we might call songs or tunes. These, he theorized, combined and were making merry, out of the earshot of man.

For Earth, he arrived at the tune of mi, fa, mi, repeated over and over again. Venus, he said, sang la, la, la in an appropriate contralto. Jupiter joined in with bass notes of do, re, mi, re, do. Thus the symphony continues today if we could but hear it.

We know that our physical ears can hear only within a certain vibratory range, and our eyes can grasp only the spectrum ranging from red through violet. Yet, the reality of music and color beyond those ranges is now established by thousands of experiments performed in scientific laboratories throughout the world.

About 400 B.C. the Greeks searched for the building blocks of matter and named the atom. As most true scientists have learned the hard way, they seldom put a period to their conclusions. And so the term *atom*, which means indivisible, has been found to be in error as modern science probes deeper into life's secrets and finds even smaller particles within the particles. Our awareness of the intelligent mind governing all life continues to increase and must continue to unfold *ad infinitum*, because the nature of the principle of life is infinite and cannot be totally defined and confined by us.

As we continue to expore our physical world, the more solid we once considered it to be the more spiritual it now begins to appear. The atom is much like a miniature solar system. Whirling in measured space like our many planets are the electrons, protons, and neutrons, with the steady white light of God-power as the nucleus. It is difficult for us to imagine an immense universe compressed into such a minute plan, governed by an order exceeding our greatest imagination.

For instance, if ordinary white light were to be broken into a spectrum a yard long, and on either end extended to include all the known electromagnetic waves invisible to the naked eye, from violet to ultraviolet, shortwave, X ray, gamma ray, and on to the other side of red to infrared, and on, the entire spectrum would be over five million miles in length.

Think now of the ever-present spiritual beauty of sound and color enveloping you wherever you are. Appreciate the fact that you live, move, and have your being truly in perfection, although it is not always audible or visible. With recent progress in human perception, life is yielding precious secrets and teaching valuable lessons. Order is one of them.

From the audible to the inaudible, from the seen to the unseen, nature entices us to visit our inner world and to relate to it. As we realize the wisdom and, yes, the humor of our Creator, who treats His children to small doses of reality, we can appreciate ourselves as the ones best able to comprehend the united kingdom by the secret door of observation and prayerful contemplation. This magical kingdom unfolds before our awe-filled eyes.

When we touch the hem of nature, we unite with the loveliness of all livingness. The businessman finds solitude, the harassed homemaker realizes peace, the timid lover finds purpose in togetherness, and thus we awaken to who and what we actually are—expressions of a Creator of infinite form and beauty that is everywhere present.

The Creator of life and love has placed His signs in earth, tree, sea, and sky. They await our awareness. From them we return to reexamine ourselves, probe deep within our consciousness, and find the same message we have found in nature. For all life is one, and the One is in all life.

Listen, then, I say, to the murmurs of nature around thee, for I say even the trees sing in tune with Me, and thy flowers murmur their praises daily to their Creator.

Flowers

Love is the unifying force of the universe. A flower's grace expresses this love which exceeds heaven and Earth. All trees, shrubs, grasses, and plants bear flowers of some kind.

Flowers grace our gardens, gladden our hearts, rejoice the fields with their beauty, and delight the wayfarer who travels the highways of the world. Red, blue, yellow, purple—they weave a colorful jewelled tapestry of petals, bells, sprays, and fringes unequaled by any other form of life.

What can be more inspiring than watching a rosebud opening to the sun, putting forth its rosy lips and sweet fragrance as it gently kisses the morning dew, growing into fullness of beauty, easing into fruition? Even the delicately tinted rose hips are beautifully carved, almost like tiny hearts pulsing with the joy of living. Roses are the symbol

1

of love from the lover to the loved one.

The rose is one of the most ancient flowers. Paleobotanists have discovered that it was abundant on Earth over sixty million years ago. Even before man made his appearance, the rose was here to greet him. A rose left its imprint on a slate deposit in Florissant, Colorado, some forty million years ago. Either the rose was planted on all continents by a foresighted Creator, or it was transplanted by man, who treasured it for its beauty.

In other words, the rose has encircled the globe. The word *rose* is in common use in English, French, Danish, and Norwegian languages. It is *rosa* in Italian, Spanish, and Portuguese, *ros* in Swedish, *roos* in Dutch, *ruz* in Bohemian, *rocza* in Hungarian, *roja* in Russian, *rosen* in German, and *rhoden* in Greek. All prove the universality of this most beautiful of all flowers.

Flowers are prime examples of reciprocity. They are love fulfilling itself, even as the poet Gibran expressed it. They provide nectar for bee, bird, and butterfly, and food for animals. They clothe the earth with beauty and provide seed as valuable food for man and beast. In return, they receive water, nourishment, and praises for their beauty and grace.

As you may have guessed, flowers began as glorified leaves, green in color. Even today we can see the poinsettia's green leaves forming the base of the flower head. Many other green flowers still exist. You probably know some of them, such as the jack-in-the-pulpit, with his cute little green pulpit neatly rolled around him like a swami's cloak in a hot summer shower, the skunk cabbage, pitcher plant, and the interesting green Dutchman's-pipe. The tiny old-fashioned curved pipes are made of large heart-shaped leaves that have been rolled and twisted into this unique design.

Slowly nature evolved green flowers into colored ones. The intricacy of their design developed as their color was added. Not all early flowers were green. Some were yellow, and all were probably very small. They evolved from green into violet, purple, magenta, red, and so on. The true blue of a forget-me-not is one of the latest colors to bless the world. I shall never forget the thrill of one hot summer's day as I came to a clearing in a New England pine wood and looked down on a small pool clustered with blue forget-me-nots.

By certain colors one can tell whether the flower species belongs to the North or the South. De Candolle invented a color system for flowers. He made two distinct groups, which he named Xanthic, the highly tinted yellows and reds found usually in the tropics, and Cyanic, the pastel blues, magenta, and violet colors of the north temperate zone.

Xanthic color is usually activated by the sun's rays. The longer the surface of a living organism is exposed to the sun's rays, the surer it is to change color. The chemical effect is generally cumulative, producing flowers of a brilliant hue that range from golden yellow, through orange, to scarlet. Thus, we observe the brilliant color of the cardinal flower, painted cup, wood lily and such, and know that these must be immigrants of long-standing whose origin was probably tropical. A flower fades because of an organic disintegration, not because the sun fades it. Sunshine does not destroy a flower's color, it enhances and intensifies it.

Just as the light of the sun enhances the color of the flower kingdom, so it is with human beings. The light of Christ removes the clouds of self-deception so we can catch the clear vision of who and what we are. When gloomy, negative thoughts of lack becloud our vision, we can remove these clouds of self-deception and see ourselves as beautiful children of God. Our true worth and identity can then shine through.

If clouds of weakness and illness tend to fade us out, let us bask in the sunshine of the Christ presence and become energized again. If we are tempted to be depressed by suggestions from the news media, we can know the Truth is that God is in charge, as surely as the flower faithfully knows

4

Flowers

the sun is there, even though temporarily hidden by a cloud.

Each family in the flower kingdom has its own identity. In order to discover which family a flower belongs to, one must take many things into account. Is the shape of the flower head bell-shaped, butterfly-shaped, a funnel, wheel, spike, or is it spurred, lipped, ray-headed? How many petals are there? And what is the number of stamens? How do the leaves grow? Are they crowded, pierced by the plant stem, whorled, alternate, opposite? Are they shaped like a sword, hairy-surfaced, round, lance-, heart-shaped, oblong, toothed, toothless, pointed, scalloped, compound, or simple? One must recognize that each family has certain juices and certain typical heights, sizes, and shapes that they follow carefully. All this is governed in a marvelous order by an unseen Mind, directing its thoughts and works with discretion and mystery. We behold the same Creator working through all of His creatures, uniting them into families with certain characteristics unique for those family members.

I well recall, back in my old hometown, families with certain traits that were common to all in that family. For instance, all the members of one family were similar in size, with certain features—freckles, and ears a bit far back. Whether or not we knew their individual names, we knew from which family they came. Another family, although they were all different, each had a large crooked nose and high forehead. How could anyone mistake them? And there was the stout, stalwart, blue-eyed family. Each family was distinctive and bore the marks of family resemblance.

We need to remind ourselves that our true identity is not something we make up. It is a divine pattern, "copyrighted" by our Creator. The rose is a rose by divine appointment, and nothing it can do can change its identity. It may grow in a swamp by the sea or on a craggy mountainside, in the shadow of a cave or in the broad sunshine, be torn by wind, driven by rain, but it is still a rose. So it is with us. We each have an individual identity. Outwardly our personalities may assume temporary changes in habit and appearance. But always we are what the Creator has decided we are, and we had best make the most of it. For the divine plan, thwarted, does not perish; it persists until we produce results. Bloom or perish!

Perhaps one of the most exquisite flowers that the Creator has blessed us with is the night-blooming Cereus. The flower opens after dark, and for this reason it is called Queen of the Night. The drama of bloom is known to hold spectators spellbound as the bud opens before one's amazed eyes to exhibit its pure, breathtaking beauty and fragrance. As many as six to eight flower heads have been seen bursting forth on a medium-sized plant.

When the owner of this special houseplant discovers a bud or buds, he or she usually summons the neighbors to go on alert. When the evening arrives for the special opening, a crowd eagerly gathers to watch the spectacle. Its haunting fragrance fills the house and remains for days afterward, even though the lovely white bloom only remains open for four or five hours and then wilts and slowly closes to go to sleep forever.

An interesting feature of this plant is that the bud seems to sprout from a long stem that comes out of a vein in a leaf. The stem is quite long, some are eight to ten inches, and quite slender. The wonder of this is how such a slender stem can bear such a huge, complex bloom that is obviously quite heavy.

I recall a summer on Cape Cod in Massachusetts when one evening the phone rang and a neighbor excitedly invited me to an opening. Since the plant blooms probably but once a year and is seen for such a brief span of time, everyone gives it full attention.

I couldn't help thinking, as I looked at the delicate stem bearing the heavy head of the lovely Queen of the Night, how much like this is human life. So many times we find delicate, sensitive people capable of bearing great burdens—family problems, marital problems, financial problems—without complaint. This is certainly an admirable quality.

The night-blooming Cereus is sometimes called the Christmas flower because the pistil spreads itself like a star out and above the circle of golden stamens that form as a cradle in the midst of such purity. The awe-inspired onlooker can readily recognize the display of purity which God has planted within the core of our being and which constantly seeks recognition in all we think, say, and do.

Have you ever smelled a fragrant blossom and found dust on the end of your nose? This dust is called pollen, and it is this important dust that must be transplanted from the anther into the pistil of each flower head. There it falls into the ovary, where it develops into ripened seeds. This process is controlled by great wisdom.

Nature provides for pollen transplant in many ways. Some flowers are self-pollinated. Visiting bees or insects will knock off the pollen from the anther into the pistil as they rummage around for nectar. Sometimes the flower depends on the wind, birds, or insects to carry its pollen to other flowers for cross-pollination. Flowers have developed certain fragrances that will attract the kind of bird, butterfly, moth, or insect they desire, and drive away those they do not like.

All kinds of ingenious ways have been invented so that flowers may become fertilized. The lady's slipper, for instance, is formed so that any insect must force its way in to get nectar. But in getting out through the small passage provided, it gets covered with pollen and carries it inadvertently to the next flower it visits. Thus, pollen hitchhikes, so to speak, from flower to flower.

Laurel is different. It has anthers that are held back by tiny pockets. When an insect of proper weight alights, the pressure of its body releases the anther and causes the stamens to spring toward the center of the flower and throw the pollen over the body of the insect. This pollen also becomes a "tramp" on the body of an insect and travels to other flowers for fulfillment.

The ingenuity of a flower to provide for the plant's continued reproduction is inspiring. For instance, have you ever walked in a summer rain and observed how the flowers keep their pollen dry? They have such clever ways, and each one differs from the others. They will twist or turn away from the rain, or even close up tightly. Watch a flower head of Queen Anne's lace. If rain ever threatens during pollen-ripening time, the whole flower bends over a couple of inches below the flower head. Wild geraniums, buttercups, and many other flowers act the same way. They droop in the rain *only* if the blossoms are ready with fresh pollen. The older heads remain upright, seeming to know that rain cannot harm them. They have already shed their pollen and have nothing to lose. Dandelions close up tightly in rainstorms, showing a natural intelligence that spells out self-preservation, one of the first lessons a child learns when it comes into the world.

There are around 200 families of wild flowers in North America, comprised of some 25,000 varieties. Most plant families have a special number. The number of petals, stamens, sepals, and leaves follows in the pattern of this number or its multiples.

Plants have certain preferences as to where they live, as do people. We may be desert dwellers or we may love to live in the woods. We may enjoy life in the wide open prairie or the icy cold of the northland. We may enjoy the sandy beaches of a mainland or a quiet island hideaway. However, we have noted the disastrous results of trying to "transplant" a city dweller to the country, and vice versa. Plants respond similarly when transplanted from their natural habitat.

All plants work toward giving their offspring a

good start in life. This is also the natural plan for humans, and those who defy it not only mar the race but bring disaster upon themselves and their offspring.

If you have ever had an ailing houseplant, you may have noticed that it puts every ounce of energy into making a bloom before it dies. This pathetic gesture of grace and gratitude is backed by its desire to give to the world its last best try toward fulfillment. A similarly touching experience has been observed by some of us as we have witnessed the struggle of a loved one close to passing, desperately trying to give his all as one last memento to those he must leave behind.

Plants *cooperate* in conducting their business of living with others. They bless the bee, moth, butterfly, and bird with their sweet nectar. Their roots help in flood control. They beautify the landscape and provide food for all living things. They are governed by a natural balance which we have disrupted with our poisonous tamperings. The imbalance of the world is not due to nature, which has always been intelligently obedient to divine law, but to man, who ignorantly threatens his own life and that of this beautiful Earth.

Much consideration has been given by flower lovers as to how much intelligence is present in a plant. Scientists are becoming involved in trying to clarify this issue, especially since a law enforcement agent, Cleve Baxter, hooked his philodendron to a lie detector to see if he could discover how long it took the water to travel from its roots to its leaves. Instead, he was surprised to find that the plant gave an emotional response. Since then, numerous experiments have shown emotional responses by plants to praise, to cursing, and even to the killing of shrimp and fish. Also, their testimony graphically shows when someone not fond of plants walks through the room.

A humorous story is told of a woman who left for a vacation and requested her unbelieving husband to talk to her plants, as well as water them. On her return, they seemed in good health. When she asked if he talked to them, he bluntly told her he read the paper aloud daily and if they wanted to listen it was up to them.

The late Dr. Richard Maurice Bucke, famous Canadian medical doctor who authored the book "Cosmic Consciousness," gives credence to a report by a woman who describes an experience she had with flowers. It was part of what he concluded to be an experience of a new and higher consciousness which eventually will lift the whole human family to a higher plane. She reported stopping alongside a shady country road one lovely morning to view a clump of purple asters. She must have been in a high spiritual state of exultation, for as she viewed them, she said the flowers began to glow with a blaze of splendor. They became like lighted gems, the color of amethysts, clear and yet with a subtle living glow. She felt they were conscious of her looking at them and were intelligently responding to her.

I recall visiting an estate one day. As I admired a certain tulip in a beautiful circular garden, the tulip actually turned its head and faced me. My friend exclaimed, "Look! That flower actually turned its head and is looking at you!" The beauty of the red tulip blurred in my vision as the life of the Creator expressed its intelligence through the lovely flower.

Another time I experienced the surprise of my life when plants were on sale in a supermarket for the Thanksgiving holiday. Passing the plant stand, I noticed a golden yellow chrysanthemum. I thought it was lovely, so I picked it up and put it in my shopping cart. After getting the rest of my groceries, I stood in the checkout line and looked over my prospective purchases. My eyes lit on the plant. I reasoned what a foolish expenditure this would be since I was going to give it to my daughter and her husband who had flowers in every room. They were in the flower business.

Hastily picking up the plant, I started to take it

back to the stand when, all of a sudden, I was startled by a strong sensation of knowing the plant was *deeply* disappointed. It wanted to be *my* plant. I stood still in the midst of the busy supermarket assimilating the experience. I also had flowers in every room. I did not need it but, needless to say, I took it home, and after the holidays it became my plant. I set it by my front doorstep where we could see each other daily.

As humankind develops a greater empathy for nature and observes more reverently the wisdom and order indwelling the flower kingdom, we will come to respect our world and ourselves more. We will notice how each plant lays aside a certain equal amount of substance for future use—not too much and not too little. Nature wastes not, nor should we. Nor does it pinch, plan, nor force. It simply tunes in to the divine will and functions in a free flow of life and beauty. How much we can learn from a tiny plant.

Following life's plan in orderly steps we, too, can meet the day's issues forthrightly, harmoniously, and victoriously. There is no problem too great that we cannot get an answer if we tune in through prayer and meditation to the great Mind of all creation. God knows; God has your answer; God cares! His intelligent love runs not only throughout the plant kingdom, it is with you now. Release yourself to Him and let His perfect plan make itself felt and known. Let every fiber of your being say to the Creator: " . . . *not my will, but thine, be done.*" (Luke 22:42) In this way, your life will increase in love and beauty, and flower into perfection.

The Good Earth

During the course of conversations with new friends regarding old friends, we often hear the remark, "Now, just how old is he or she?" This question has also been posed about Earth. Just how old is it?

Geologists have come up with a variety of answers, but anthropologists are now finding ancient remains of man's activities on Earth that push the date of Earth's origin back further and further. A general guess as to the age of Mother Earth might be three to four billion years. This information is gathered from geologists who study uranium in rocks.

Earth is about seven-tenths water and three-tenths land, so we can see why there have been so many changes and shifts over these many millions and billions of years. Water is the moving power.

As Earth rotates on its axis completely once every twenty-four hours, it also circles the sun. The revolution around the sun is what constitutes a year, or 365 days, six hours, and nine minutes, to be exact. If we were to thrust a sword through the center of the planet, we would have to have a very long sword. It would need to be almost eight thousand miles long.

We can diet and keep our weight down, but not so with Earth. Although it weighs some six sextillion tons, its weight increases yearly from a constant shower of cosmic dust that adds close to two million tons annually to its weight. What chance does Earth have but to increase until it becomes a cosmic elephant? All joking aside, we know this, too, must be in the Creator's plan.

We will speak about the seas and fossils and animals of Earth later, but we need to remember that the planet which bears them is composed of three main ingredients: land—the solid ground, water—the liquid substance, and air—the gaseous substance. All the substance of Earth, and that of the universe, is God's substance, a part of His eternal body, because there has been nothing but God from the beginning. The Bible tells us: *In the beginning God* . . . . (Gen. 1:1)

Since we are made in the image and likeness of God, and made out of the very substance of God, and Jesus told us that *"God is a Spirit,"* then we are spiritual creations, whole, perfect, and beautiful in every respect. It is now up to us to claim, in the name of Jesus Christ, the perfection that is truly ours for the good Earth, for the birds, the trees, the animals, the fish of the seas, and the fowl of the air. *And God saw everything that he had made, and behold, it was very good.* (Gen. 1:31)

Note that when God surveyed His handiwork, He did not decide that it was fairly well done or partly good, it was *very* good. So we can know that we have inherited a stupendous, glorious place in God's handiwork, and it should be a privilege and a pleasure to be a dweller on this beautiful Earth.

But, I hear you ask, how did this all begin? Again, we turn to the Bible and read: *And God said . . . .* (Gen. 1:3) God spoke after He had thought very carefully. When He spoke, it was something like a gigantic atomic explosion of universal magnitude. The Psalmist caught a mild hint of the magnitude of this happening when he wrote, speaking of God: *. . . he sends forth his voice, his mighty voice.* (Psalms 68:33)

The theory being advanced today by scientists suggests that everything began at once with a great burst of power and energy. How close can a scientist come to God before he admits God? Many outstanding, humble scientists are acknowledging the presence of a power greater than the universe that has created all things and is maintaining control of all things.

Not only did God create Earth, He also made it a vast storehouse so that our every desire could be perfectly met. Water, sand, and large land masses have risen and sunk over billions of years. Glaciers have crawled over the land and then receded, leaving deposits of mud, sand, gravel, and rock, carving out great valleys and sculpturing cliffs and mountains. Earth continues to change, although the change is slow and does not meet the eye of the casual observer. The past is the key to the present, and the present is the key to the future. Rocks, hills, seas, fossils, and land masses leave tales that have been recorded in many history books.

As life appeared on Earth, rotted vegetation, animal matter, and leaf mold added substance to sand and gravel, and loam was formed to host the more delicate forms of plant and animal life. The garden of Earth was being prepared for God's masterpiece: man.

In God's storehouse, He placed tools to help man evolve into the glorified being he is destined to be. We shall all be changed: *For this perishable nature must put on the imperishable, and this mortal nature must put on immortality.* (I Cor. 15:53)

Weathering attacks of wind, rain, ice and snow, heat and cold, and various pressures, together with erosion, landslides, and ocean waves gradually formed three main types of rocks: igneous, sedimentary, and metamorphic. Igneous rocks are formed from hot, molten liquid masses known as magma. When these masses cooled, they formed hard, igneous rock. This is sometimes called *bedrock* because it lies beneath the surface and supports other forms of rock such as sedimentary rocks. Sedimentary rocks are rocks made up of particles of sand, pebbles, or other rock particles derived from preexisting rocks that have broken down and formed layers which have hardened with time.

Metamorphic rock is the third large family of rocks. These are rocks that have been changed from their original form by earth pressures, heat, and chemically active liquids beneath Earth's surface. These rocks may have been made from changing a sedimentary rock into a new and harder formation. The study of earth-substances is a deep science, and we are barely touching on it. But, if you are interested, you may read further by obtaining books on geology, weather, soil, and so on from your local library.

People who have never studied Earth are amazed to discover that change is a constant process. It is much like when one of our friends, a chief executive of a large company, recently retired. He was presented with a beautiful Shaker rocking chair. He was instructed to sit in it and begin enjoying it. This he did, smiling with pleasure. But soon he got up and thanked his friends, saying, "If you think I'm going to spend the rest of my days in a rocking chair, you have another think comin'!" He let it be known that, although he would indeed enjoy his rocker, he meant to use his retirement years for meaningful soul development. Of man and of Earth one thing is certain, and that is *change*.

As change took place and rocks were formed, vast stores of iron, lead, copper, and other valuable metals formed underground. Gold and silver appeared in veins. Oil formed in massive pockets and wells; coal formed as plants; trees and ferns rotted and turned into peat. Then as land masses sank, and oceans poured in carrying sand and mud and pressure, coal was formed. Coal is still forming in some places even today.

Coal is sometimes called *buried sunshine*, because when we burn coal, we are burning the energy that was captured from the sunlight as it fell on the ancient forests which turned into coal long ago. Coal, as you well know, is a popular source of heat and is found in most countries throughout the world. Almost half the world's supply of coal is located in the United States. The amount of coal mined in a usual year in the United States is enough to fill a train that would circle the Earth at least three times.

I can recall visiting a large coal mine in Nova Scotia and sitting in the forsaken coal miners' car that had carried them down into the "big hole." The cars were abandoned because there were so many cave-ins and so many lives lost over the years of mining that the mines had to be closed. As I sat gazing down into the void of that black hole which wound deep into the bowels of the planet, I felt that certainly miners must be praying men.

The life of a miner is a difficult one. Many people had spent their lifetimes at this occupation and were able to save enough money to buy a small house on a tiny lot of land. Now that the mine was closed, they were faced with the problem of owning a house no one wanted to buy, and being without a job. We prayed for them and trusted God to work out a satisfactory solution.

Time, water, pressure, and winds all played a part in sculpturing Earth's surface into mountains, plateaus, caves, deserts, plains, and beautiful landscape. We all enjoy visiting Arizona's Monument Valley with its tall, jagged rock spires, Bryce Canyon, Zion National Park, Yosemite, Walnut Canyon National Monument, and, of course, the Grand Canyon—all masterpieces of nature.

In the beginning, when Earth was first created, it is believed there was constant volcanic eruption. Earth cooled and took solid form, the volcanic action lessened and became so rare that whenever an extinct volcano erupted, it was a spectacle that caused scientists to rush to the site to study it firsthand. In recent years there have been an increasing number of worldwide volcanic eruptions which are responsible not only for our bizarre sunsets, but some are believed to have affected the windows of the larger planes of Scandinavian Airlines System. Because of window glazing, the System has had to begin a program of replacing the windows in its airlines.

When the particles causing the fine scratching effect were analyzed by chemists, it was found that particles of aluminum, sulfur, and silicon were present and appeared identical to those thrown off in volcanic eruptions. These particles drift toward the arctic region at around 40,000 feet, which is the cruising altitude of jets. Here again is Earth affecting atmosphere, and the atmosphere retouching objects of Earth. The cycle continues indefinitely.

No one can stand and gaze at the changing panorama in the Grand Canyon and not become awed at its beauty and grandeur. Orange, yellow, gold, bronze, deep purple, pink, chartreuse, mauve, and rose—all unfold before one's eyes in an ever-broadening view.

Mammoth Cave of Kentucky, Luray Caverns of Virginia, and the vast Carlsbad Caverns of New Mexico were carved by ancient underground rivers. Now they are filled with beautifully formed and delicate stalactites and stalagmites. Here is an underground world of rivers lost in antiquity with limestone icicles. I will never forget my excitement in visiting these caverns.

Later, I experienced a similar excitement when I picked up a round, smooth stone, broke it open, and discovered that within it was a miniature cave displaying glistening amethyst crystals. The crystals which form within these geodes are usually some variety of quartz, although calcite or dolomite crystals are sometimes found in them.

Geodes are formed when a water pocket develops in a sedimentary deposit. A silica shell forms around the liquid, and by a process known as *osmosis* the crystals are formed.

Rocks are made up of minerals; minerals are composed of crystals. There are six primary systems of arrangement for crystals. The term *axis* is a word that mineralogists use to express the inner force fields that are present in all crystals. They serve to orientate a crystal as it forms its outer geometrical symmetry. It is marvelous to realize that crystals of each mineral family can usually be counted on to occupy precisely the same positions in space. There are only four different kinds of axes of symmetry among the world's crystals. All minerals are formed on definite mathematical laws. The beauty of design found among them is awe-inspiring.

When a mineral is melted, it becomes liquid. This is because matter is made up of atoms and their molecules. As the material melts, its molecules, which before stood in solid form like soldiers in a row, leave their places and move around like men who have broken rank.

Minerals turn into gas under great heat. Then their molecules fly away from each other like an army in panic. Interesting things take place in a chemist's laboratory.

You have, doubtless, crossed over a railroad bridge. Of interest is the fact that the steel beams of these bridges may gradually change and become crystalline, thus losing some of their original strength because of the molecular arrangement that has been damaged by the vibrations caused by the constant jarring of passing trains. These beams have to be periodically replaced.

Since all life on Earth is subject to atomic structuring, we can easily understand the impact that musical vibrations must have not only on our minds but on our physical bodies. If vibrations can shake a steel railroad bridge apart, we would do well to select the music we listen to with care. Noise pollution has become a serious threat to many major cities throughout the world.

You probably remember the early radios, fondly termed *crystal sets*. My daddy had one, and I can remember him hovering over it with earphones clamped to his head, intently listening to "First Nighter." When the crystal died, or whatever it did to wear out, Daddy simply took a walk and found another fine quartz crystal on our farm to replace it. The atomical content of the crystal was able to connect with the receiving part of his set in such a way as to be completely miraculous to me.

Dr. Donald Hatch Andrews, past professor of chemistry at Johns Hopkins University, was an interesting friend who knew much about what went on inside the atoms of a mineral. In his fascinating book *The Symphony of Life,* (now out of print), he concludes that intelligent action appears to be everywhere constantly present. According to Dr. Andrews, the atomical action that takes place in plants, trees, flowers, birds, fish, and, yes, even "dead" rocks is excitingly revealed as an intelligent, ordered swirl of color accompanied by glorious orchestrations. If we could only hear this, it would probably transform us into new dimensions of experience. Occasionally one hears of someone who has contacted this eternal dimension of sound and beauty, and he or she finds it difficult to report about it in human terms.

On a small island in the midst of beautiful Lake Winnipesaukee in New Hampshire, our interesting friend and scientist, Dr. Andrews, used to share with us what he called his "atomic music." Seated at the piano in the old boat house, his nimble fingers would roam over the keys creating sonatinas, minuets, and fugues based on the frequencies of certain atomical vibrations brought down to our level of hearing. With that we would be transported to new realizations of life and beauty heretofore unknown to us.

If such music and color were taking place inside the atoms of our own bodies, what about the gray granite rock upon which our cabin sat? Or the handful of pebbles we saw Dr. Andrews scrutinize one day? "Yes," he affirmed, "they all sing and dance."

"And the flowers and grasses and trees?" we queried.

"Those also," was his reply.

"Then it is a perfect, beautiful, singing world," we said, and knew the Psalmist was correct when he wrote:

. . . the hills gird themselves with joy,
the meadows clothe themselves with flocks,
the valleys deck themselves with grain,

they shout and sing together for joy.
(Psalms 65:12, 13)
And again in the Bible we read:
Let the floods clap their hands;
let the hills sing for joy together.
(Psalms 98:8)
Did the Psalmist surmise an inner world of light and joy, or was he gifted with an increased awareness that permitted him to tune in to such high frequencies? In a day and generation where daily breakthroughs in awareness occur, one can well ask such questions.

Inorganic substances such as rocks and gemstones, although inanimate, also evolve according to law and order. They are composed of various chemical elements, each with its atomic formula, and the same intelligent universal law that controls the common destiny of animal, vegetable, and man also controls them. What shall we call it? Some call it God.

Many have been fascinated by the beauty of famous gems on display in the Tower of London. A trip to the dark tower on a misty day will reveal the blue of the sky, the flame of a sunset, the glory of a rainbow, and the brilliance of evening stars perfectly captured in gemstones. All proclaim the exaltation of an inner kingdom beyond the manipulation of man, the kingdom of God, which we inherit as

God's beloved children.

The Morgan-Tiffany collection of gems and the Morgan-Benoit collection of minerals, the exhibits in the Smithsonian Institution in Washington, D.C. or the Musée d'Histoire Naturelle of Paris, and other famous displays show the ingenious art of a Creator who has captured the loveliness of a fading petal or the perishable flash of a firefly, and set them as monuments hidden in the earth—temporal treasures around which the petty schemes of man are woven. Trying to possess such beauty, men and women have fought and died. Yet the beautiful, free, living essence of this is with us all. How beautiful is a human life that has come to realize this and constantly express such beauty.

From the beginning of time, gemstones have attracted the attention of humanity. Many precious and semiprecious stones are mentioned in the Bible. You might enjoy looking up the following references: Genesis 2:11, 12 mentions onyx—a flat, layered, striped mineral in different shades of color, excellent for use in cameos. Exodus 28:15-20 mentions the beautiful stones ornamenting the high priest's breastplate. The stones were set in four rows: a sardius, topaz, and carbuncle, then an emerald, a sapphire, and a diamond; and third, a jacinth, an agate, and an amethyst; and last, a beryl, an onyx, and a jasper—all set in gold. Each

stone was engraved with the signet of one tribe of
the Children of Israel. Job 28:18 mentions crystal,
which we all admire; and in the nineteenth verse of
this same chapter, topaz is spoken of as coming
from Ethiopia. And the pearl is spoken of by Jesus
as being a symbol for the kingdom of heaven.
(Matt. 13:45)

Chinese emperors of the Manchu dynasty wore
yellow girdles ornamented with precious stones.
The lapis lazuli, a purple-blue stone, was chosen
for the ceremony in the Temple of Heaven. Yellow
jade was chosen for the Altar of the Earth. We
know of the special love of the Chinese for jade.
Jade in different colors was used in their worship of
heaven and earth, and the four cardinal points.
Jade was often carved with signs, symbols, and
figures, and the museums of today hold many
treasures of antiquity.

The ancient historian, Pliny, tells a story of a
marble lion with emerald eyes. This lion was set
near the tomb of a petty king called Hermias, on
the coast. He told how the fish were frightened
away by the flashing emerald stones, to the utter
disgust of the fishermen.

Folktales passed down by centuries of retelling
mention an only ring worn by St. Valentine in
Ireland. The ring contained a lovely amethyst with
an engraved cupid. This, it is surmised, was a

pagan gem worn by this pious Christian who assuaged his conscience by bringing the Christian meaning of love to bear in it. Whether or not the legend is fact or fable is left to conjecture.

In 1831, Maharaja Runjit Singh, ruler of the Punjab, had his portrait painted. In this picture, the Maharaja is shown holding a long strand of large polished emeralds made to look like beads. Doubtless, these stones were not so rare in his day as they are today, but they still held great value for their beautiful grass-green loveliness.

The American Indian has a special love for turquoise, making rings and mosaics out of it. These stones are gradually becoming harder to find in the high quality that used to be so plentiful.

Diamonds have always attracted attention. Even birds like diamonds! In Golconda, for instance, a once-fortified town of open diamond mines in South Central India, the birds picked up diamonds that lay on the surface of the ground and swallowed them. Later, people found these stones in the birds' nests and in their droppings. How would you like to find a diamond-studded bird's nest? The birds know a good thing when they see it!

The famous Kohinoor diamond, or Mountain of Light, was also found at Golconda. This very large diamond was used as tribute to establish the Mongol Empire in India. It was owned by many

men, and finally came into the possession of
Mohammed Shab. He hid his precious jewel in his
turban, but a member of his harem learned of the
secret and told another man, Nadir Shah, about it.
The story goes that Nadir Shah held a feast and invited Mohammed to exchange turbans under the
pretense of swearing eternal friendship. Needless to
say, much blood was shed to possess this finest of
all jewels.

The Kohinoor diamond finally came into the
possession of Great Britain and was taken to
England when the British annexed the Punjab in
1849. We can imagine the elation of young Queen
Victoria, thirty years old at the time, wearing this
magnificent jewel in court.

It remains part of the British crown jewels. There
is a model of it in the tower of London, but the real
gem of some 106 carats is held in security in Wind-
sor Castle.

A beautiful story is told of another large diamond called the Star of the South. This diamond
was found by a slave who used it to buy her freedom. What price freedom? It later sold for 15 million dollars. This is said to be one of the highest
prices that has ever been paid for one person's freedom. Freedom is priceless, as we all well know.

The largest diamond recorded from early discoveries was called the Cullinan. It was found in 1905

in the "blue ground" of the Premier mine in South Africa. Blue ground is a term referring to the bluish color of the soft rock that contains the diamonds. It is believed to be volcanic pipes, and the diamonds in it are connected with the eruptive outflow from underlying rocks.

Diamonds are judged by their weight (carat), flawlessness, color, and, later on, their cut. The Cullinan weighed 3,025 carats (over one-and-one-third pounds) on discovery. The Transvaal government purchased it and presented it to King Edward VIII of England. The stone, in turn, was turned over to gem cutters in Amsterdam and cut up into nine large stones and ninety-six smaller stones. The largest of these stones still holds first place and bears its original name, Cullinan I.

The Jonker diamond was later found in 1934 and was said to be of such flawless purity that it was unequalled by any other diamond of its size. It weighed 726 carats. After it was cut up, it made twelve flawless stones. Besides these famous gems, there is also the Dresden diamond, which is a lovely green in color, the Florentine diamond, which is a beautiful orange-yellow color, and the famous Orloff, a part of the Russian crown jewels. This stone was bought by Prince Orloff and presented to Empress Catherine II. Legend has it that it formerly was set as an eye in a Hindu idol, and through a series of hair-raising episodes, the jewel came into the possession of the royalty of Russia. It was cut into an unusual shape as diamond cutters experimented to discover the shapes that would give the greatest brilliance to each stone. The style of cut seen most today was begun in the 1600s and is called the *brilliant* cut. It is round and has fifty-eight facets (faces).

The famous blue Hope diamond was large when found, but thieves stole it, and later it appeared about half the size of the original stone. After an exciting history, an American, Edward B. McLean, purchased it. It weighs forty-four carats. Another famous diamond is the beautiful Regent or Pitt, regarded as one of the most beautiful large stones. This stone may be seen on exhibit in the Louvre Museum in France. Other famous diamonds are the Sancy, Polar Star, Shah, and Eugene.

Industrial uses have been found for the diamond. It is used as a glass cutter, in abrasives, and in the bits of diamond drills. Since it heads the list in hardness, nothing except a diamond is hard enough to cut a diamond.

Although diamonds are now produced artificially, they do not possess the perfect refractive index or structure of real diamonds. Under the X ray, a real diamond proves itself by becoming transparent and is easily discerned from a glass imitation.

Despite the fact that diamonds are the hardest natural substance in the world, they are quite brittle. A sharp blow can shatter one easily. If diamonds are heated without oxygen, they turn into graphite, the substance used in lead pencils. These mystery stones bring rainbows from beneath the earth to meet with the splendor of rainbows in the eyes of a betrothed, and rainbows in the skies. God's wonders never cease!

Although diamonds were discovered early in India in open stream beds, India produces few of them today. Brazil is a second producer, while Africa leads, producing over ninety percent of the entire world's supply. Diamonds are found in places such as Borneo, where they are associated with platinum, in Australia, and in the Ural Mountains.

Stones in small quantity have been found in the United States in the gravel of North Carolina, Georgia, Virginia, Colorado, California, Idaho, and Oregon. Between two and three thousand stones have been found in Murfreesboro, Arkansas, in loose soil and peridotite rock. I remember the thrill of roaming, for a small fee, in the soil looking for diamonds. One of my friends found a diamond of considerable worth, had it cut and polished and set in a ring. The price of the entire ring in no way equaled the fun of finding her own gemstone.

A yellow diamond of 511 carats was found in 1951 in South Africa, and a flawless blue diamond of some 426 carats was found there in 1954. It pays to keep one's eyes open since all these discoveries were unexpected. As the saying goes, there may be "gold in them thar hills," and there may be diamonds in your own backyard.

Another group of gems that are well-known are those that belong to the corundum family. These are next in hardness to the diamond. Among these lovely gemstones, we find the beautiful blue sapphires and red rubies. These compete with grass-green emeralds in costliness. The ruby that is pigeon-blood color is the kind that is most greatly valued.

Many interesting stories surround gemstones and their great worth. At times a large, perfect ruby may be worth several times more than a diamond of the same size. Both rubies and sapphires are also made synthetically, and it is difficult for a gem dealer to discern the difference.

Crystals take on strange shapes deep down in the dark earth. Sometimes they are close copies of the shapes of flowers, birds, snowflakes, clouds, stars, and cobwebs found on the upper sunlit surface. Nature seems to repeat her patterns over and over again in the different kingdoms. For instance, the mineral known as staurolite has crystals that resemble stars or crosses. Moss agates often have the clouds of the sky pictured in them. Crystalline structures of cinnabar, scarlet red to slightly brownish in color, can sometimes resemble seaweed, while dolomite, white and often tinted rose red, can crystallize into what appears to be a beautiful rose.

Azurite, with its crystalline fringes, resembles the purple aster that clusters by the wayside in autumn when the leaves turn to gold. The mineral wavellite could almost be a sand dollar the children pick up at the seashore. Pharmacolite has fuzzy, fluffy-looking balls of crystals that resemble a full-blown thistle.

Silver is often found as irregular masses of fine wires that resemble cobwebs. The next time you are at a jeweler's, look carefully at the opals, and perhaps you will detect the shadow of a bird flying into a sunset of flame and purple.

Certainly Mother Earth has provided many luxuries for us. Jewels may be the most precious. Because of our love of the beautiful, birthstones have become popular. Garnet is worn for January, and amethyst for February. March is bloodstone or aquamarine. April is the uncontested sparkling diamond. May is emerald or pearl. June's stone is moonstone. July is the beautiful red ruby. Peridot or sardonyx is the birthstone for August, while the lovely blue sapphire is the gem for September. Opal or tourmaline is the birthstone for October, November has the golden topaz, and December has three stones that may be chosen—turquoise, zircon, or the purple-blue lapis lazuli.

As Earth turns, it colors its seasons and years with festoons of jewels and garlands of flowers and green growing things. How truly did the Psalmist write: *The earth is the Lord's and the fulness thereof, the world and those who dwell therein; for he has founded it upon the seas, and established it upon the rivers.* (Psalms 24:1, 2)

And again: *Bless the Lord, O my soul! O Lord my God, thou art very great! Thou art clothed with honor and majesty, who coverest thyself with light as with a garment, who hast stretched out the heavens like a tent, who has laid the beams of thy chambers on the waters, who makest the clouds thy chariot, who ridest on the wings of the wind . . . Thou didst set the earth on its foundations, so that it should never be shaken.* (Psalms 104:1-5)

O Lord, how manifold are they works! In wisdom hast thou made them all; the earth is full of thy creatures. (Psalms 104:24)

Water

What is more beautiful than a body of water glistening in the sunshine, reflecting an azure sky, gathering its nourishment from a mountain stream? We all enjoy bathing in such a lake, living close to its edge, and even drinking from it. It is a wholesome body, blessing all life around it. It is directly connected with its source of good and shares that good with others. On the other hand, water that is shut off from its source becomes bitter, stagnant, and eventually poisonous.

In similar fashion, people who are conscious of their divine source sparkle with joy and enthusiasm. They are men or women who give the most to life and receive the most from it. On the other hand, the one who, like a stagnant lake, closes himself off from divine communication becomes a dull, uninterested being, severed from the life that created him, nonproductive to those around him. He is a whited sepulcher, of which Jesus spoke, that wilts beneath the relentless pressure of problems that attach themselves to those unprepared for their mastery.

Have you ever leaned over a quiet pool and observed your face mirrored below? Water reflects our state of being. Here we see the Truth of God revealed by the camera of mind's eye. Here we behold the problem and its answer. Here we see the strengths and the weaknesses, and resolve to do something about them. How wise is he who holds on to his true reflection and attempts to bring it forth in more perfect outer ways.

As well as being beautiful, water is essential to all life on this productive garden planet. So essential is water to our welfare that we seldom can go beyond ten days without it. If we were to examine our bodies, we would discover that the liquid part of our blood is ninety-two percent water, and the rest of our body is composed of eighty percent of this precious liquid we take so much for granted. Although we are surrounded by leafy trees, lawns, and plants, it is a watery world. All life must have water in order to exist.

Water provides power for industry. Its force is constantly re-sculpturing the landscape. It removes large masses of rock and earth to new areas, builds up hills, and levels others, washes away bankings, creates valleys, changes coastlines.

An example of how water changes land formations may be seen in the awesome spectacle of the Grand Canyon. As one looks across the vast expanse with its rocky cliffs changing color moment by moment, and faintly sees below the great Colorado River appearing as a tiny trickle, one can begin to imagine the handiwork of water in the hands of its Creator.

Springs flow into brooks, brooks flow into mighty rivers, and rivers into the ocean. The great seas and mammoth oceans cover almost seven-tenths of the entire planet, and should all the mountains and hills be leveled and the depths raised evenly, it is estimated that the earth's water would spread over the entire world to a depth of some 8,000 feet. As one stands on the seashore and awesomely considers this, he must unite with the Psalmist who questioned his Maker: *What is man that thou art mindful of him?* (Psalms 8:4) What, indeed?

Can you remember how refreshing it was when you last stopped by a wayside spring to drink of the cool crystal liquid gushing from the dark depths? Cold springs ripple forth from what appears to be an inexhaustible source of supply. Not far from our home is a cool spring where folks may take a jug, walk across the slippery, mossy planks and, by bending low beneath the fragrant hemlock branches, fill it to the brim. On a hot day one may often see a traveler quenching his thirst from this fountain of the deep.

The great Atlantic shimmers in the eastern sun. Great ships glide upon its surface, while beneath, in the clear waters, salts and minerals are constantly at work purifying the refuse that nations pour into it. We are just beginning to recognize the valuable properties of ocean water and its elements.

We are told that half a billion years ago, possibly during the Cambrian Age, the ocean's waters were one-third as salty as they are now, and they contained the minerals and salts in the same proportions as our present human blood. Here we can see a connection between organic and inorganic substances and the sense of oneness enveloping all creation.

The tempestuous Pacific pounds upon the shores of a million beaches, buoying up the surf riders and those with arms outstretched as they float upon the crest of a wave. Sailing craft and swimmers alike accept its buoyancy.

Did you ever dive into a high breaker and come up on the other side with a mouthful of salt water? We are cautioned not to swallow it, as it is detrimental to our health. Yet occasionally one reads of a shipwrecked person who was stranded for hours and days in a lifeboat on the ocean, dying from thirst and not daring to drink the salt water around him, but who did not know he was caught in a fresh-water river, maintaining its own identity, wending its undiluted course through the midst of the salty sea.

We can be like such a river and remain undisturbed by raging storms, polluted conditions, or massive negative circumstances around us if we will continue to be daily united with our source of divine life and direction through prayer, Bible reading, and meditation. While others are in confusion, we can calmly know the path to follow and be about the Father's business. Thus, we retain our own free individuality, yet still are part of society.

Have you ever noticed how you are drawn to certain individuals and not to others? There is a law of attraction that is active throughout all forms of nature. It was Sir Isaac Newton who discovered in the 1600s that the moon and sun must affect Earth's water level because of the force of gravitation. Before that, the early naturalist Pliny, around the year A.D. 100, believed that the moon influenced the tides. Now science has been able to calculate with accuracy the movement of the tides, the tide cycle being about twenty-four hours and fifty minutes, generally speaking.

The gravitational pull of the passing moon affects the water nearest it, while at the same time pulling Earth a little in the same direction, away from the water on the other side of the globe. Then, tidal currents are active on the opposite sides of the planet at the same time. The motion would continue to travel around the Earth. The only thing that stops the tides is higher ground.

All bodies of water on Earth are influenced by the gravitational pull of the moon. But it is so minor in the inland lakes and streams as to be unnoticeable. Lake Superior, although a fair-sized body of inland water, has a tide of some two inches.

In contrast to this, the Bay of Fundy in Nova Scotia is famous for its very high tides, there being a difference of some forty feet between high and low water averages. The range averages more than fifty feet at the extension of the Bay at the head of what is known as Cobequid Bay. I first visited there on a camping trip with my two daughters after my husband's passing. I recall the feeling of alarm at seeing the waters come in so swiftly and so high onto the shore.

Tide times never change. Since they are so dependable, ship captains use tide tables much as the Canadian National Railway uses timetables. The land along most sea coasts has two tides every day, occurring fifty minutes later each day.

There is great therapy in listening to the sound of the breakers on a sandy shore, or the gentle lapping of wavelets against a canoe in a lake on a moonlit night. There are gifts memory can store until we can again experience the water music first-hand. If you are troubled, seek out a quiet place near the water and let the good Lord heal your nerves with the soothing sound of the water.

He hath compassed the waters with bounds, until the day and night come to an end. (Job 26:10 A.V.)

There are many qualities about water that make it a unique substance. One of them is surface tension. This is a kind of elasticity that serves to contain water in droplets, such as dew upon a blade of grass. This quality also allows for the control of the water's edge, maintaining a defined outline on the seashore, lake shores, rivers, and waterways. Without this elasticity water would be quite uncontrollable.

We also must exercise elasticity in response to life's stresses, and take command of them as opportunities to provide order in our lives. Thus far and no farther is the rule of water, and it is a very good rule for us to follow.

Water seeks its own level, even as we do. We constantly strive, as children of God, to find our natural level—one where we may use our particular talents and abilities and where we may feel the thrill of fulfillment.

Order, being heaven's first law, also applies to water. It is one substance in three varying forms, all perfectly controlled by nature's higher laws, blending with the rest of life. At a temperature above 212 degrees Fahrenheit, it is in its gaseous state called steam. At this point, its molecules are widely dissipated. Between 212 degrees and 32 degrees, water is a liquid, and its molecules are closer together but moving about like a herd of cattle. When the temperature is below 32 degrees Fahrenheit, it manifests its solid state, which we call ice. Here the molecules are arranged in perfect order by the mind of our Creator, like ranks of soldiers.

Ice is perhaps the most unusual solid in existence. Most solid states are heavier than their liquid forms and will sink to the bottom when placed in liquid. Water is one of the rare substances that is less dense than the liquid from which it is formed. This allows it as ice to float in its own liquid. Were the solid state of water heavier than its liquid, ice would soon form a solid mass that would annihilate plant life and living creatures. Most of the world's water would then become gradually solidified—a solid, cold, dead body. Life in the world would soon disappear, and the world, with the exception of the tropics, would turn into a cold, damp, crusted mass of uselessness. But the loving, wise Creator thought of this and prepared the way for all life to continue in its evolving course of oneness.

Water readily releases itself to the will and plan of the Infinite. As you watch it glide over twigs and branches lodged in its path, ripple under obstructions or around boulders, you can catch its nonresistant manner and its harmony with all creation. It gives drink to the thirsty flower that droops by the wayside, nourishment to gardens and lawns, and spreads a banquet of multi-flavored juices and foods that would delight a king.

How easily we can accept the lessons of water as we nonresistantly release ourselves to the will and plan of the Father, and find our true place in family life, business, or community affairs. Even as water flows happily, without effort, to its destination, we may move effortlessly in harmony with all life around us.

The next time you see water seeping through sand or stone, know that if the Creator can do this with water, He can do this with your problems. He can infiltrate them and help you solve them. On your next trip to the beach, watch a child building sand castles. Watch his amazement when an unexpected rivulet of water seeps in and the castle wall dissolves. So we, like happy children, are relieved to find the presence and power of Spirit at work in our lives, pulling down strongholds, dissolving problems, bringing health, harmony, peace, and supply wherever needed.

If you are ready for another water lesson, some hot summer day try driving to the country. Walk between the jack-in-the-pulpits and trilliums to a little brook, and stir the water with a stick. What happens when the muddy brook is stirred? The accumulation of the past slowly washes away. Often the mud doesn't rise to the surface but is carried away at a lower level. So it is with us, the Lord's tender forgiveness often heals at a subconscious level, and the one healed never knows what particular problem was removed. He just feels gloriously cleansed and free!

As you watch the mud flow quietly downstream, remind yourself that you are even now giving your accumulated problems to God for Him to wash away. Even as water disappears under a bridge and is never to return, so your problems now disappear, never to return.

The little stream, the lake, the ocean give themselves to sun and air, to creation itself. Their moisture is carried out and up, and condenses as rain, to fall again at some appointed place and time. And so the cycle continues for the benefit of all. As recorded in Matthew 5:45, the Father

" . . . sends rain on the just and on the unjust."
God's gifts are given to one and all of His children
without favor or discrimination. The apostle Peter
once told the followers of Jesus: *"God shows no
partiality."* (Acts 10:34) He loves us equally.

Listen carefully to the raindrops the next time it
rains. Notice how not one falls at the same time as
any other. Each droplet at its independent time
unites with the whole effort of blessing. If raindrops were not divinely timed by a responsible
Thinker, can you imagine the damage of one single
rainstorm as all drops thundered down upon objects in one solid mass of weight? Nothing could
survive for long.

Listen, dear one, to the music of the raindrops
that a responsible Creator has arranged for your
therapeutic help. The sound of rain calms the emotions, washes away fear, encloses you in a liquid
crystal of love and security. It brings harmony to
frayed nerves and solitude to the weary. Raindrops
play melodies so pure and beautiful no one has ever
captured them.

Much like raindrops, life has a divine timing and
natural rhythm. Inherently we all recognize this
and, sooner or later, we strive to accept what is
natural for us. We can be too early or too late for
appointments, speak before we should, or be slow
with an important comment. All action has divine

timing, and happy and successful are those who find it for themselves and abide by it.

Even as we can water down certain substances by diluting them to become ineffectual, we can water down our own naturalness. How many people do you know who water down their lives with restless activities that neither contribute to that person's well-being nor enhance it? Sometimes one will observe a gifted writer, painter, or musician frittering his time away on trivialities rather than disciplining himself by observing the true value of time and effort. Or we might see someone milling around without aim or reason, doing what is easiest for the sake of earning money, without ever questioning, "What is the purpose for my life?"

As each drop of rain has purpose, so has every one of us been born for a purpose—a purpose that fits into our individual plan for happy fulfillment, and that meshes with the universal plan for the peace and progress of society. No one is an island. No one was born for misery or failure. All of us are God's beloved children, and each of us has a part in His overall plan for life as surely as each musician in an orchestra has his part in producing a symphony. The violin is needed as much as the cello, or the bass viol, or the cymbal, or the bassoon.

Your "instrument" is unique. Like the raindrop that gives itself to the rain, or the little river that provides substance for the body of the great sea, you have a specific purpose and can contribute something different to life that no one else can. Thus you are unique, even like the crystalline form of water as it freezes into a beautiful snowflake. No two snowflakes are the same. This is an awesome statement when one considers the hundreds of trillions of snowflakes that fall on the polar caps yearly, and those that fall across the entire globe.

A Vermont naturalist by the name of Bentley spent much of his lifetime photographing snowflakes. (We will discuss snowflakes later.) Through his studies, he found that nature always has a plan and an order and that there are certain types of flakes or families. So we might say water has family identity, even as do birds, flowers, insects, fish, animals, and yes, even man.

And so we find from the very nature of water that it is natural to have order in one's life. It is natural to be in harmony with life and to be flexible, flowing with the current but avoiding those troublesome problems by meeting them and moving quietly and peaceably around them, under them, or by lifting them up into the light and blessing them. It is natural to be uniquely different from every other person. Yet, it is natural to be a comfortable part of society and contribute our individuality to life as one beautiful whole.

The divine plan is patterned throughout nature. We reach out and explore, seeking to find differences, but we return home having discovered that differences lead to sameness—sameness in lesson but not in application, oneness in the One, yet oneness in diversity.

Tennyson wrote of the brook:

> I come from haunts of coot and hern,
> I make a sudden sally,
> And sparkle out among the fern,
> To bicker down a valley.

*   *   *

> With many a curve my banks I fret,
> By many a field and fallow,
> And many a fairy foreland set
> With willow-weed and mallow.

> I chatter, chatter, as I flow
> To join the brimming river,
> For men may come and men may go,
> But I go on for ever.

Sea Life

Gifts from the sea

The story of sea life and its relationship to all life on Earth is well-known, but let us touch on it and reawaken our interest. It was Goldsmith who said: *People seldom improve when they have no other model but themselves to copy.* The more we consider nature, the more we can appreciate the wisdom of God moving with precision throughout all things, bringing the world into divine focus and ultimate meaning.

O Lord, how manifold are thy works! In wisdom hast thou made them all; the earth is full of thy creatures. Yonder is the sea, great and wide, which teems with things innumerable, living things both small and great. There go the ships, and Leviathan which thou didst form to sport in it. (Psalms 104:24-26)

The age of manifest sea life dates back billions

of years. Its primal history is written on sedimentary rocks, as sea creatures were created, lived, died, and their remains became fossilized in layers of sandstone and shale. Fossils of plants and animals, both from land and sea, have been found near seacoasts that give us a picture of the different early life forms as they related to one another then, as compared to their forms of today. Geologic time is divided into eras, periods, and epochs. The interested researcher can find books bringing him through the Paleozoic Era, Mesozoic Era, and Cenozoic Era to the present forms of sea life.

While visiting the ocean, most of us have seen jellyfish, a very early form of sea life. Sometimes these soft-bodied creatures are stepped on or kicked while swimming. Most of them have interesting markings in their gelatin-like bodies, and children are fascinated with them when they happen to be cast up on the beach.

The jellyfish, called the Portuguese man-of-war, is actually a hollow bladder filled with gas, which allows it to float on top of the water. This raft is populated by tiny sea animals, each with a unique job to perform, much like sailors sailing a boat. They are free riders, and their job is determined by each one's structure. One will find food for the crew, another will protect the colony from invasion, another will propagate the colony. From beneath the man-of-war hang streamers sometimes fifty feet long that are highly poisonous to humans and sea life. In this way the jellyfish traps its food and is nourished.

During the Cambrian Period in the Paleozoic Age, five of the major divisions of present sea life existed: sponges, brachiopods, mollusks, segmented worms, and arthropods. Seaweed, sea cucumbers, trilobites, sea lilies, corals, starfish and sea urchins were counted among these early forms.

Perhaps you have picked up a pretty starfish or a sea urchin etched with lovely designs. Sea urchins are called pin cushions by people who see their close resemblance to them. Others think they look more like doorknobs. The skin is covered with limestone plates. Underneath, the urchin has a large mouth. The small hole at the top of the shell is to allow the animal's eggs to emerge. The dots on the shell are the locations of tubes that may be thrust out into the water to suck up small animals, which it then draws into its large inner mouth. These tubes also double for feet when the creature navigates in the sand near the shoreline or in deep water. We usually see these creatures when their tubes are withdrawn, but when they are out, they can look like full-blown thistle heads.

Seaweed comes in many colors and designs. We are all acquainted with the large brown or red or green ribbons that are tossed up on shore during a storm. A form of algae, these are relatives of the green pond scums we find in stagnant water.

The famous Sargasso Sea in the Atlantic Ocean east of Florida is clogged with masses of floating seaweed which often slows sea traffic. On Columbus's first voyage to the New World, his ships had to pass through huge masses of thick seaweed. This type of floating weed is sometimes called gulfweed. It has air bladders shaped like tiny footballs. The shores of the Atlantic coast often display this dark brown-to-black seaweed, and children enjoy squeezing the tiny footballs to hear them pop.

It is interesting to note that agar-agar seaweeds are the red variety of algae classified as gelidium. It is sometimes called Ceylon moss and is found in tropical Asia and on the Pacific coast of the United States. It is used in making Oriental soups, jellies, and medicines.

Kelp, another form of seaweed, is found in both the Atlantic and Pacific Oceans and is often harvested for fertilizer and explosives. Kelp is also used as a body conditioner, since it is rich in vitamins and minerals. In the olden days, kelp was burned to obtain ash for soap making. Today it is valued as a good source of iodine, which varies from five to fifteen pounds per ton.

Land masses have risen and lowered into the sea

as time has elapsed, leaving a coral reef in the state of New York, and coral off the Gaspesian coast of Canada, when waters there were once tropical or semi-tropical. Recent findings by geologists in Canada have brought amazing discoveries to light, and rare fossils have been found along the shoreline.

There is some question as to whether the monster of Loch Ness in Scotland may be left over from past ages when the seas covered that area of land. I recall standing on the shores of the Loch on a dark December day, hoping the monster would surface so we could see him. But it was not to be, and we had to take the monster as fact or fable. It is believed by some that sonar soundings have actually located such a creature. It is amusing to see some of the pictures drawn by people claiming to have seen him. Most of us would not relish waterskiing on the Loch, I'm sure.

A somewhat smaller sea creature is the dolphin. You have probably been entertained by their performance at various aquariums throughout the country. They are a friendly type of whale that travels in schools. They love to perform for people by arching their backs and leaping into the air, diving, and playfully chasing each other. Once killed for its oil, flesh, and leather, it is now somewhat protected by those who realize it is a creature of high intelligence. It was considered sacred by the early Greeks, and many poets have written about the dolphin. Jesus said that man had eyes and saw not, had ears and heard not. Today, we give thanks that our eyes and ears are becoming open to the wonders God has richly stored around us.

There was a story in the newspapers written by a young woman who claimed God used dolphins to save her from being eaten alive by sharks. She was vacationing on a cabin cruiser headed for the Indian Ocean. As they drew near, a freak storm with thirty-five foot waves hit them and sank their cruiser. One man drowned, and the rest clung to life jackets and each other.

At dawn, she decided, since she was a strong swimmer, to swim for help. She estimated that she must have swum about nine miles when she found a marker buoy. This gave her hope. Then hope was dashed as she spotted six sharks around her. They had been attracted by the blood from a cut on her foot. She prayed aloud, "God, please, You must help me. Please help me!"

Miraculously, God immediately answered her by sending two dolphins that swam along, one on either side of her, protecting her from the sharks. Whenever she began to sink from fatigue, a dolphin would give her a nudge to keep her swimming on. When she tried to touch them, they veered away. As she climbed up on the buoy for safety, the two dolphins swam away. She said she cried for the first time, as she felt two of the best friends she had ever had had just left her.

On her return to Pretoria University, where she was a student, she reported the incident. Word got to the Oceanographic Institution in Durban, South Africa. The director, Dr. Alan Heydorn, admitted that the story did not surprise him too much, as dolphins have been known for many years to befriend human beings in trouble at sea. She has called the two dolphins her "sea-angels."

Among the outstanding creatures that live in the sea are the sea lions and seals. Seals, although docile and friendly by nature, are not very intelligent. Those seen on shows are usually California sea lion cows that show considerable intelligence. They can be trained to play a tune and can be seen playing ball with seaweed or driftwood, throwing it up and balancing it on their noses.

The fur seals were killed for pelts so persistently that the herds had dwindled to less than 150,000 when the United States signed a treaty in 1911 with Russia, England, and Japan and took charge of the herds. Even with the treaty it was necessary for the United States to patrol the area, and in this way the herds have been built up to over a million.

Seals provide the Eskimos with food and oil for

light, heat, and cooking. The yearly harvest of skins is around 70,000.

A sea creature that has attracted quite a lot of attention is the small sea horse. It is named this because its head looks like a horse's head. The rest of its body grows up to ten inches long, sometimes smaller, and it ends in a tail that can twine around objects. After the female sea horse lays the eggs, the male tenderly cares for them in a pouch on the underside of his body until they hatch. Baby sea horses are so petite many of them could get inside a thimble. Gift shops sell quantities of dried sea horses, as well as seashells.

The world of shells is another area of sea life we should explore, for there is such variety of color, form, and beauty one can hardly exhaust it.

The chambered nautilus has become famous from a poem written by Oliver Wendell Holmes. In recent times, this shell has been singled out by mathematicians and artists who are studying the Divine Proportion or the Golden Section portrayed by the school of Pythagoras. One study includes a radiograph of the shell and claims that the successive chambers of the nautilus are built on a framework of a logarithmic spiral. As the animals increases its shell, the size of the chambers increases, but the shape remains perfectly the same. They have found a pentagonal symmetry in marine animals. It is claimed that these same proportions are found in the King's Chamber and the Great Pyramid. Analysis of the proportions of a human skeleton also follow this divine plan. Sir D'Arcy Thomas calls the Golden Section, "Gnomonic Growth." Actually, it is a succession of numbers in geometrical progression or a succession of similar shapes. We must admit that the beautiful rhythm and design of the chambered nautilus is a perfect example of the Creator's simple elegance.

The creature begins life by building a single chamber. Then it adds other chambers, each one larger than the one before but in the same proportion. With each addition, the nautilus seals off the last chamber and moves into the new one. Some shells have as many as thirty chambers. This shell is found in deep, warm waters of the Indian Ocean and the South Pacific. It is a mollusk, like a squid, and has about ninety tentacles that it uses to catch its food. It is perfectly protected, of course, when it withdraws into its shell.

If you come across a shell that resembles a snake, it is called a worm shell. Sea worms live inside. In contrast is the beautiful abalone, valued for its pearly luster and loveliness. Interestingly enough, it breathes by extracting oxygen from seawater!

Most of us are well-acquainted with scallop shells. At least 200 species of scallops are available.

They navigate by opening and closing their valves rapidly. The muscle that makes this jazzy motion possible is the delicious part that humans love to eat. The shells come in a great variety of combined colors, and some of the pink, yellow-orange, and purple combinations are exquisite. It is an amazing fact that nature has a way of combining colors that complement each other. When humans try to mimic her, the results are often gross and jarring.

One of the common, pretty shells is the tiny coquina. They are little butterfly shells, so-called, with colors ranging the rainbow. It is impossible to find two alike, and the rainbows seem to be without end. Florida beaches abound with them.

The oyster is quite a strange sea animal. The oyster has three brains or nerve centers. With one, the creature feeds itself by opening its shell and filtering tiny food particles out of the water. Another center controls its vital organs, and a third brain center utilizes oxygen. The oyster changes sex many times during its lifetime, from male to female and back again. When a single female oyster releases some 115 million eggs in a cloud at sea, the male sheds his sperm at the same time, and the fertilization of the eggs takes place in the water. The baby oysters look like tiny pebbles with streamers. They come equipped with a special glue so they can attach themselves to a hard surface and begin the process of growth.

If a grain of sand gets into an oyster and cannot be expelled, the oyster begins defensive action by coating the grain with thin layers of a mother-of-pearl substance (nacre), and a pearl slowly takes form and shape. If an oyster can make a thing of beauty from an irritation, how much more should we be able to bless our difficulties, turn to God, and let Him make good out of them.

The conch is one of the most famous shells, since we all like to pick it up and place it to our ear to see if we can hear the roar of the ocean. The knobbed pear conch is probably the most well-known and is the largest snail found along the Atlantic coast north of Cape Hatteras. Its egg cases look like curious coins strung on a long chain. When they are washed ashore after a storm, they become dry and are like tough parchment. Inside each parchment disk are tiny baby pear conch shells.

The giant conch is the one with the pink interior exposed to public view that is prized for decoration. It is a scavenger and hops around on the ocean floor, making long skipping leaps when frightened. Semiprecious pearls are sometimes contained inside this shell.

We are all acquainted with the cowries found in the Pacific Ocean and the pretty wentletraps with their lovely spiral peaks like whipped cream. Last but not least is the triton's trumpet from the Indian Ocean and Japan, which is used as a trumpet by some Pacific Island tribes. This conch is collected on the beach and can serve many uses: water vessel, teakettle, pan, or basket.

Do you know that the sea sometimes makes patterns on the beach? Two of my friends reported that one day they were walking on the beach, and there at low tide near the waterline, in clear weather, were long rows of trees etched in the wet sand. These trees had trunks and branches, and the pattern extended for about ten to fifteen feet, parallel to the waterline, with the trunks facing the receding water. Within the overall picture were several parallel strips of the tree design, each strip about a foot deep and separated from the next strip by several inches. Was this nature's special art show for the day, or was it caused by the crystalline structure of the sand or the molecular action of the water? We never saw the sight again, but we are still looking.

What fun it is to go clam digging! I had the opportunity of accompanying some professional clam diggers in Maine one day. Patiently they waited for the tide to go out. When the tide was close to the low-water mark, they quickly got into their boats with their hip boots on, taking pails, clam-forks, bags, and the rest of their equipment. The small fleet of boats motored out to the mud flats, off-shore by about a mile. By then the tide had gone out about as far as it was going to go.

We all scrambled out of the boats and dug as fast and furiously as possible. The clams were abundant, and by the time the tide had changed and began to make us sink in the sand, we had a large quantity of food to take back.

Back on shore, some of the families enjoyed with us a delicious steamed-clam dinner. A fire was built in their out-of-door pit, lined with native rocks. When the fire got very hot, the men ceased stoking it. The clams were spread out on the hot rocks, covered with wet, salty seaweed, and permitted to steam until they were cooked. These were served with baked potatoes and melted butter. It was a feast fit for a king!

Most beach lovers, while strolling along the Atlantic beaches, pick up bits and pieces of jack-knife clams. Occasionally, we will find one whole. This reminds us of a parallel to people, tossed in the waves of life. Some are broken by the force of conditions, but others are able to float along, at peace with their surroundings, centered in the God-power within. Such individuals are admired by us all. They have come to know their oneness with God, and have developed faith in His power to save them from undue stress and strain. They live in harmony with the circumstances that come their way, and find the good that they know God can and will surely produce in accordance with their faith. Such are the giant characters of history. But each of us can learn the lesson of letting God's love buoy us up through times of trouble, even as the seashells are carried effortlessly on the crest of the wave before they alight on the shore.

The giant clam, Tridacnidae, is the largest shelled mollusk found in the Indo-Pacific. It lives in the coral reefs and feeds on colonies of marine algae. It is next in size to the giant squid of the North Atlantic, which is also a mollusk.

A visit to one of any of the many shell shops in Florida or the Gulf Coast is a treat. Here we find shells gathered offshore by divers or by dredging. The shapes, designs, and colors provide a wealth of beauty for the nature lover. Perhaps the eastern American Murex shells are among the loveliest. They are fluted, twisted, and fringed with projections, some of them exhibiting a lacy appearance. They have been named Lace Murex.

Back in the days of the Phoenicians and later, the Greeks and Romans coveted Murex shells for the purposes of dye making. Their woolens and cottons when dyed by the juice of this creature, attained a permanent purple, called royal tyrian purple. Such cloth brought high prices and was valued by royalty. Roman emperors and senators wore this color to signify their rank and importance. After the fall of the Roman Empire, the Christian Church at Rome used the same dye for the robes of Christian cardinals.

One could go on and on, remarking about the treasures of the sea. Not only does the sea cast its treasures at our feet, but it provides food in many forms for us to eat. We, in return, owe responsibility to the sea to keep it clean and unpolluted. As more effort is being made to clean up our waters, nature will, in turn, continue to produce that which is needful for our well-being.

Our discussion of sea life would not be complete unless we mentioned some of the birds that love the sea and live on it. Perhaps the arctic tern is one of the most interesting in that it lives in the waters of the land of the midnight sun. The arctic tern may be the bird that can fly the longest distances of any bird in the world. When winter comes, they leave their breeding grounds in the northernmost part of the world and follow southward to the southern tip of Greenland, eastward to the shores of Europe, and then south by the west coast of Africa to the South Atlantic. Some terns fly 22,000 miles to Antarctica, where there is again perpetual sunlight. They are known as the sunlight birds, and even when they strike a darkened place, they behave as though it were light. As the Psalmist said: *: . . the night is bright as the day; for darkness is as light with thee.* (Psalms 139:12)

Shorebirds include sandpipers, ducks, avocets, and stilts, plovers, phalaropes, guillemots, and puffins that look like clowns. The only colony of Atlantic puffins nests on Matinicus Rock off the coast of Maine. At mating time, their bills take on colors of bright red, yellow, and blue, giving the bird a comical look.

Their neat black backs and white tuxedo fronts bob along as puffins walk. Short, stumpy wings are used to propel them underwater to catch fish. A puffin is a good fisherman and can catch as many as twenty-five fish on a single fishing trip. How it manages to hold one fish in its mouth while catching another is hard to comprehend. As the jokester remarked, ''You said a mouthful!''

After the mating and nesting season is over, the parent birds lose their bright colors, and their bills return to a black color as they prepare for their winter flight. Their winters are spent at sea. No one seems to know just where they go. In late March, the lighthouse keepers see them returning to nest again in Maine.

The sea gull is cousin to the tern. We are all familiar with these lovely birds soaring through fog and over white-capped waves, with white on their chests and heads, and with pearl-gray markings on their wings.

Richard Bach, in his beautifully inspiring book, "Jonathan Livingston Seagull," mentions a sea gull school where the young gulls are taught to improve their flying skills. I had taken this part of the book lightly until one October I happened to be staying at a cottage on a northern beach. The days were getting cool and crisp, and a hint of winter was on the edge of the wind. For hours I had the privilege of observing a flock of sea gulls, on a deserted strip of land behind the dunes, instruct their young in the art of intricate flying. Older birds would perform delicate twists of the wing, deep, sudden swoops. Soon the young birds would follow. Over and over various wing tricks were practiced until the next instructor took the "floor" and began the next step. I presume each flock along the coast was preparing its young in a similar way for the approaching winds of winter. It was interesting to hear the calls of the instructors as the young birds, clumsy in flight, faltered or failed to maneuver correctly.

Another rare experience occurred while I was on the Gaspé coast in Canada. A group of us had decided several weeks in advance to hold a special meditation on a particular mountainside. At the appointed day and time, we were in our places on the mountainside, where we prayed for the world and were just settling into meditation, when I observed a strange thing taking place.

In the field far below us a gull flew in and came to rest. Then another, and another, and another. They took up positions in complete silence and seemed to be waiting for others, which soon flew in from all directions. Each gull settled into place, with four birds stationed at the four corners of the flock. There they all sat in complete silence, without moving, for the entire hour we spent in our meditation. Then, as we broke silence, so did they. They moved around, appeared to be bidding one another adieu, and off they flew in the various directions from which they had arrived.

Our group was amazed at the procedure. A sharp lookout was kept on the field, for we thought it might be a favorite resting place for sea gulls. But they never came again. Were they also meditating? Do birds meditate? It seems strange to even ask such a question, but we know so little about what goes on in the great sea of life around us that if we continue to ask questions and become involved in more personal research, we may come closer to some real answers.

Sea gulls are very community-minded. They appear to have rules and regulations set up for rulership of the flock, and they definitely have a pecking order. If one sea gull is eating a piece of fish that someone on a boat has thrown overboard, and another gull comes along of superior pecking authority, the first gull gives place to the second. If the second gull is down the pecking scale, the original gull continues eating his fish. Gulls are the scavengers that clean our coasts and eat what other bird refuse to eat. Quantities of gulls will follow after a ship and wait for the ship's kitchen to throw overboard the refuse of the day.

Wheeling and crying, gulls bed down for the night on the rolling waves and are literally rocked to sleep in the "cradle of the deep." As the sea lends its body to the life it sustains, so in turn, that life lends its help to the body of the sea.

We say with great respect and praise, O Lord, *thou art great and doest wondrous things, thou alone art God.* (Psalms 86:10)

Birds

Humming bird
M. Russell

What is lovelier than a Baltimore oriole flashing his beautiful black and gold coat among the pink and white apple blossoms? Or a pair of yellow canaries darting from one painted daisy to another? Birds spread the beauty of their bright plumage for us to enjoy.

Faith is the bird that feels the light and sings when the dawn is still dark, observed Tagore. It is thrilling to listen to the first songs of the day as the birds wake from slumber and praise the Creator for the passing night.

At noon the birds again sing and give thanks. Who among us does not enjoy the birds' sweet evening carols of humble benediction for another day of life under the sun? In faith, we too can give thanks to our Creator morning, noon, and night for the good we expect to receive and the good we have already received. Faith has moved many a mountain. Faith works as surely for us as for birds.

The writer of Proverbs declared that there were three things too wonderful for him, and one of these was the way of an eagle in the air. (Prov. 30:18, 19) If one is fortunate enough to spot one, it is a thrilling sight. With their mighty wings they can soar high in the sunshine and blue skies, while storm clouds wrench the trees with wind and rain below.

In similar fashion, it is inspiring to see a person who is filled with spiritual strength soar above life's stormy problems, maintaining a peaceful attitude and a tranquil approach to life.

Have you ever wondered why the Maker created birds? Is it for their beauty or songs, their diligence as predators, their balancing of nature, or their usefulness to humankind? Or is it perhaps all and more than these?

Birds made their appearance much earlier in Earth's development than did the flowers. Some 120 million years ago, the first birds were giant flying lizards with bodies covered with scales. They had wings twenty to twenty-five feet from tip to tip, bony heads and powerful jaws, sharp teeth, clawed feet, and four legs. They resembled bats as they suspended themselves upside down in the great trees of that era. Fossil remains tell us much about these prehistoric flying creatures. Nine million years ago some birds were seven feet tall, while others were the size of pigeons of today.

When man arrived, birds were here to greet him. Because of their strangeness, men ascribed certain omens to birds. The ancient Aztecs who saw an eagle sitting on a cactus with a snake in its claws considered it a good omen, and they built Mexico City on the site. To this day, the symbol remains on Mexico's flag. The bald-headed eagle is the United States' symbol of courage and strength. Utah's Salt Lake City has a monument to the sea gulls that appeared at a time of crisis in response to prayer, to devour millions of grasshoppers that were endangering Mormon existence.

One of the joys of visiting the woods is to listen to birds' songs. How still is the redwood forest without the song of birds! There are no parasites on the trees there, so birds visit other woodlands for food. In fields one may listen to the meadowlark, or by the swamp to the red-winged blackbird clicking its warning or giving forth its trill. Some birds, like the song sparrow or mockingbird, have many songs. Other species, like the robin, sing only one or two. But in most cases, the male does most of the singing. Each species of birds has its specific call, and by careful discernment one may tell if the bird is from Canada or the United States. There is a

difference as surely as a Frenchman speaks French
and an Englishman speaks English.

Apparently, though, different species of birds
can communicate with each other. For instance, experiments show that when a dangerous owl is present, songbirds call to each other, using a call that is
quite different from their usual song, to recruit the
necessary number of birds to drive the enemy away.
Their sharp, repetitive tones even draw our attention, and we can witness how they not only call,
"Help is needed!" but tell the others *where* it is
needed. Divine intelligence works in so many ways
yet unknown to us. Scientists who are studying bird
songs may some day discover some unexpected
sidelights on how humans acquire speech.

Song is a special gift from our Creator. Not only
birds sing, but wolves often howl in musical choirs.
Crickets produce song in the grasses by rubbing together a file and scraper located on their forewings.
The humpback whale sings in the great sea a pro-
longed and slurred trumpeting. And we all enjoy
the chorus made by spring peepers. The ability to
rejoice and sing praise is given to every living creature in one way or another. As we observe nature,
the barriers melt, and we feel at one with all
creatures.

Birds often flock together and gain certain bene-
fits as surely as do people who cooperate as fami-

lies, cities, or nations. Birds can find food more easily in flocks because they give clues to each other as they fly. Each bird maintains his individual personality, however, and this is recognized by the rest of the members of the flock. Each has his place and priority in the flock, from the head bird down to the least. This avoids waste and arguments. So when Mr. Headbird arrives, all other birds step aside and let him feed.

After many years of observation, we are only beginning to learn about birds. Their migratory patterns still amaze us. For instance, before cold weather comes, how do they know when and where to fly? When warm weather approaches, what makes them return again to former nesting sites? What wisdom guides tiny birds all the way from Florida to a certain farm in Maine that has a barn waiting for them in which to raise their families? We used to have barn swallows who were certain to arrive on the sixteenth of April. We were so sure of their arrival date, we would remove the barn window only the day before, every year. Are there lighted highways in the skies invisible to us? Are there signs and calls passed from flock to flock as they pass each other from north to south? Are there certain natural airflows that are used to ease the long passage from country to country? Are there specific feeding grounds that are en route and part of the knowingness of a bird? Some will tell you they know these answers, but much of it is still guesswork. Naturalists are learning more about such things with new, improved equipment.

One day while I was playing a recording of a bird song, a tiny bird flew up close. She was sure her mate must be calling, and she was responding to his call. The lovemaking and courting displays of birds are quite entertaining. The male prairie chicken, for instance, puts on an amusing combination of antics and dancing, puffing out his chest, making noises, spreading his tail feathers and strutting, stooping, saluting the female. Male penguins, on the other hand, are most matter-of-fact. They simply toss a pebble, and if a female picks it up, there is a wedding.

Birds claim certain territories, and their reasons for territorial rights are well-founded—they make no excuse for it. It may be to protect a mate, a nest site, or a lookout site, a food source, breeding area or courtship space, a covey, or even a display ground.

It is entertaining to observe swallows as they make their daily lineup on a telephone wire. Watch what happens when one tries to squeeze in. He is either rejected and must fly elsewhere, or he wedges in and the whole line makes a fast readjustment.

There are many ways of comparing the ways of a bird with the ways of humans. For instance, the screech of a bird, as the shout of a man, can be an announcement of territorial rights. There are degrees of warning. The first says, "This is my place! No loitering here!" The second may say, "Leave my wife and family alone!" The third may warn, "If you get any closer there will be a show of force to prove that order prevails here!" Humorous or not, we must admit that the nations of the world are organized in similar fashion, each respecting the rights of others and expecting reprisal should an infringement be made. Thus freedom is exercised by respect for territorial rights—*a first law of nature.*

The wisdom governing the bird kingdom is amazing. For instance, what man or woman is born knowing how to build a house? But each bird knows what materials to use, what pattern to use, how to form them successfully, and where to locate its nest!

Housing for birds differs greatly according to species. Their nests are found in brackets in chimneys, in gravel pits, hanging saddle fashion from tree limbs, or on the ground. Some are baskets woven of roots. I shall never forget finding a tiny hummingbird nest, long after the birds had left for the South. It was such a small thing, hardly larger than a woman's watch, woven of fine grass and hairs, and carefully wrapped with spider webs. Upon this, gray lichen was carefully stuck for beauty. It was lined with the softest, downy chaff of ferns. What tender love was expressed by such a home!

And so we find a bird preparing for her little ones with the greatest of care, even as a human mother prepares the bassinet and layette for her child. The father and mother bird love each other and wait upon each other, work together, feed one another, and care for the eggs together. When a mother sits on the nest, the father feeds her and sings to her his most beautiful songs.

When the time comes for the eggs to hatch, how is baby going to work its way out of the shell? Will Mama kick the egg out of the nest and smash it to liberate her young offspring? Or will Daddy fly by and drop a pebble to give the egg a gentle crack? Neither is necessary, for lo and behold, baby has grown an "egg tooth," a spike on the tip of his beak! But see what happens when baby is hacking the shell away and a dangerous predator is near. At the sharp warning cries of the parents, the baby ceases pecking and remains quiet until the danger has passed.

All this takes place before the baby bird has met his parents. What invisible, unheard rapport exists that is prenatal in birds? Surely a similar rapport exists between the human mother and her unborn child. How careful the new-age pregnant mother is to protect her child and give it only love and devotion from the moment of conception.

Some ducks have nannys or baby-sitters for their young. Recently, while sailing on a northern lake, we watched a single lady merganser leading a group of nine or ten babies on a water stroll. She is to entertain and feed them all day and safely deliver them to their various parents at day's end. When Mama and Papa fly in from a day's work, Nanny comes with their two or three children.

How do Mama and Papa know who will make a good sitter, and how do they arrange for an orderly morning pickup? Is she paid by some extra delicacy, or does her reward lie in a job well done? Life holds many questions that may never be answered.

Even as a human mother prompts her child to brush his teeth, comb his hair, or take a bath, so adult birds train their young in good grooming. There is a daily bath, either in water or dust. Then the bird flies to a handy branch, gives its feathers several strong ruffles, and begins a careful preening of its feathers and skin. The routine is as follows: head feathers are cleaned by a scratching foot, the bird turning its head so that the toes can scratch the crown, sides, and chin; flight feathers of the wing are cleaned by the bird's grasping the feather near the base and drawing it through the bill in one steady jerk. After preening is complete, the bird anoints its feathers with oil. The preen oil is taken from a small gland located at the base of the tail. Thus its raincoat is in order in case there is stormy weather.

And speaking of stormy weather, have you ever thought about putting birdseed or suet out for the winter birds when the snow and sleet make foraging impossible? This is not only a kindness to our bird families, but it can turn into a very interesting pastime.

One family we know has a bird feeder on the railing of their back porch within easy view of the breakfast nook. Each morning they are entertained by their beautiful visitors, and as the weeks pass, they recognize certain old friends among them. Occasionally there appears a stranger among the chickadees, sparrows, or blue jays. One never knows who might show up for dinner!

There are various ways to make bird feeders that are simple and effective. For instance, a soap shaker filled with suet can be easily hung from a twig. You are then in for a treat, as you wait to view the tricks that follow. White pinecones can be easily tied to a branch, and when dabbed with peanut butter, they provide a tasty lunch for hungry grosbeaks. A metal soap dish with springs on each end will tack up easily against the garage and safely hold suet. Used orange or onion bags can also serve this useful purpose. The snow bunting loves nothing better than to come across a feeder full of seed ready to be quickly devoured, providing a blue jay is not on the scene. Blue jays have a reputation for being the loudest, rudest, greediest birds around.

The downy woodpecker gives good account of himself as he stays around orchards, keeping up a tireless search for insect robbers of fruit. When cold winter winds begin to blow, he is well-prepared with a warm coat of fat under his feathers and a cozy pecked-out cavity in some nearby tree. When he moves out in the spring to find his mate and raise his new family, nuthatches, titmice, wrens, tree swallows, owls, or crested flycatchers often move into his forsaken quarters. Each one helps the other with little thought about having done so.

In my growing-up years I became interested in birds through the blackbirds that visited my daddy's kitchen garden. Mother would help him make man-sized scarecrows, stick figures dressed in human clothing that would flap in the breeze to scare the birds away. It was believed then that the birds thought the figure was a real man and did not dare go near the garden. However, it is considered now that any moving object is a threat to the bird's safety and they may even be smart enough to know the difference between a stick figure and the real thing.

The cousins to these greedy birds, the red-winged blackbirds, nested in the beautiful meadow below our home. Every spring they returned, and it was always a treat to walk in the fields in the evening and listen to their vesper songs—sweet, serene, true to pitch and full of well-being.

A bird is an instrument of God to bring peace to man. The song of a bird brings no taint of anxiety or worldly concern. When a bird sings, he gives his all to making *a joyful noise unto the Lord*. His song is always true to the notes given to his particular family from the great Creator. He seldom varies but is on pitch, in tune, and obedient to the call. How much we can learn from this! Through obedience to the Lord, man has received all the good things due him. Through disobedience, man has maimed and disabled himself.

A recent report came to us regarding this particular kind of bird, the red-winged blackbird. They are easy to spot with their flashing stripe of red on their wings as they dart quickly about their business. A flock was noticed in a western town. It must have been toward spring when there was still ice in the ponds, or in the small water locations. The report tells us that this particular flock gathered around a puddle in the road to get a drink, only to find it frozen over. Several of them tried to open the pool by pecking at the ice with their bills to no avail. The ice proved too thick to penetrate. Apparently, they were all thirsty and were aware of it to quite a degree of intelligence. We have no way of knowing how information is passed between birds in the flock, but it is obvious that they do communicate within the body and often act in a united way to accomplish a precise purpose for the well-being of the entire group. God expresses His intelligence through every living thing, and birds are no exception.

The observer of this particular flock told us that one by one each bird flew down to the ice and laid its body against the ice. At first the spectators thought the birds were injured, but after a minute or so the bird flew up into the air again and another took its place. After this occurred many times the ice was apparently melted sufficiently for them to approach the puddle en masse and busily peck together until an opening was forced and they all got a drink. Such incidents almost indicate a reasoning capacity.

Here is a beautiful lesson in sharing. As each one shares some of what he has to share, the whole is benefited. Why are we so often prone to withhold the good that might benefit someone else?

I recall a woman secretary who had to dress well for her job, praying about what she called her "poverty-appearing wardrobe." Through prayer, she was led to act in faith and have compassion for another woman or two or even three in her neighborhood who did not fare as well as she did! With a sincere feeling of goodwill, charity perhaps, and loving concern for their happiness, she approached each one and offered them one of her better dresses, saying she expected to receive some new dresses herself. Would they like to have the ones she was disposing of? Each woman gladly received her gift and blessed her for it.

The fact of the matter was that our friend did not have any way of knowing where she would ever get more dresses to replace those she gave away. She was acting on pure faith, knowing that as she liberally shared what she had to share God would surely fill the void and bless her. I must add that her faith was rewarded. A week or two later she received an unexpected pay raise and was able to renew her wardrobe in a good way. The emphasis of the whole exercise was not to get, however, but to share that which she already had to share. In doing so, the whole neighborhood was blessed and made happier.

This is but a small example of the power of sharing. Many people share from their wealth or surplus, few share from their want. But if each of us shares what we have to use in whatever way God instructs us to, we find ourselves becoming involved in many wonderful ways that bring joy to us and others. It has often been said that if each Christian would share generously with others what he has been given, the world could be changed overnight: . . . *freely ye have received, freely give.* (Matt. 10:8 A.V.)

Have you ever wished you were as free as a bird as you watched one swoop and sing in the air above you? The form and grace of a bird in flight is greatly to be admired. Seldom do we consider the art of flying an achievement. Somehow we think a bird is born knowing how to fly, able to keep itself braced in the gales, or able to drift with ease on a calm wind current. Yet learning to fly is a great accomplishment for each bird.

The thought of flying apparently makes young birds quite fearful. If you have observed them learning to fly, it is much like a small boy learning to dive off a diving board for the first time. The bird will shift places, look the other way, and pretend he doesn't know what he is supposed to do. He will stall until the shrill coaxing of his parents becomes so demanding it must be obeyed. Drawing in a deep breath, the wee bird leaves the perch and flaps its wings for all it's worth. Mother bird prompts its actions, even as a human mother directs her child in the swimming pool. "Hold your head up, Darling! Keep your arms moving! Watch out for your feet!" These are no doubt similar instructions to those given the baby bird in bird language.

I'll never forget the amusing scene of a family of barn swallows. Each baby bird lined up on the window ledge with Mama behind them, demanding they get into motion. Papa was out front, demonstrating how it was to be done, calling instructions and urging his offspring into action. One by one the babies took flight, and fluttering, returned, flustered like a young girl after her first date.

All but one learned to fly that day. We called him Buster. Buster clung to the perch with a death grip. Nothing was going to get him off it if he knew it first! The fact that his brothers and sisters had made it did not persuade him in the least. He did not want to fly, and that was that. He would walk on terra firma! But that was not the way of a bird. He was scolded by his parents and taunted by the other young birds, all to no avail. The next day passed, and he still sat there. I'm sure if he had had teeth they would have been firmly clenched. Surely his bill was. He looked very glum as evening came.

The third day at exercise time, the baby birds again tried their wings, excitedly flapping and fluttering up and down around the farmyard. But Buster sat firmly grounded on his perch. He accepted his morsels of food along with the chiding of the rest of the family. As afternoon approached, Mama and Papa could stand it no longer. They were just as determined that Buster should learn to fly as he was determined he would not and could not.

With great arguing in shrill voices, they coaxed, pleaded, and then grew angry. It was almost as though one could hear Papa say, "See here, Buster, I'm fed up with you. Now get moving!" With that, he swooped down behind Buster, knocked him off his perch, and continued to fly under his body, supporting him in the air, as Buster, scared to death, began flapping his wings for dear life. That day Buster flew, and from then on the family progressed in peace and harmony.

How often we see a similar situation in a human family. Perhaps there is a family effort needed for one who hangs back, unwilling to participate or determined to spoil the fun for the rest. There comes a time when love must take a firm stand and uphold the good of the whole.

A man who seemed to be a very ordinary person confided in me one day that he had always wanted to paint. He had not had an opportunity to do this as a child. He had to begin earning a living at an early age. As we talked, he realized it is never too

late to begin to develop an inner desire. He signed
up for a drawing course. After he learned to create
a good composition, he took watercolor lessons. He
soon became better than his teacher. People seeing
his pictures offered to buy them. Little by little he
spread his beauty around and is now a prominent
hobbyist who displays his paintings at fairs and art
shows. Not only has his talent provided a lucrative
and pleasant way of service, it has also drawn out
his interesting characteristics and developed him
into a well-rounded individual.

At times we are all "Busters." There are things
that must be done that we postpone, or there may
be new experiences we need courage to tackle. We
hesitate and look the other way, and as we wait, we
can almost hear Buster calling to us, "Spread your
wings! Try it, Brother. You may even like it!"

Trees

In Genesis 22:18 (A.V.) we read the words of God to Abraham: ... *all the nations of the earth be blessed; because thou hast obeyed my voice.* The remarkable ability of Abraham to prayerfully discern the Lord's will and obey it contrasts to most of us who consider ourselves capable of going along under our own steam. Why should we take time to listen, meditate, or pray and talk with God? Because when we go out on our own, so to speak, we reap the unmanageable consequences of our own unbalanced decisions.

Nature, on the other hand, is able to maintain balance and provide proper nourishment and beauty for all when left on her own. But nature becomes unbalanced by the tamperings of man. Man, divinely directed, is successful. Man, self-directed, manipulates himself and his world into difficult situations from which it is impossible to back out. The truth has to be eventually faced, and repairs often go back to the beginning of the mistake. There are few shortcuts in nature.

Trees are a fine example of what happens when a living organism is allowed to obey its inner promptings. Perhaps this is why Joyce Kilmer likened a tree to prayer. The grandeur of his statement of how the tree looks to God and lifts its leafy arms to pray is demonstrated everywhere. Walking through a city park, we can see a stalwart oak or horse chestnut with its branches raised upward in an attitude of adoration.

Science has recently detected growing sounds made by vegetation, which makes one wonder if trees actually pray. Is all creation praising the Creator? Only God knows the order and meaning of such phenomena. It was Carlyle who said: *Prayer is and remains always a native and deepest impulse of the soul of man.*

Trees bless the Earth with their beauty. Trekking through wild country, the hiker stops occasionally to view a colossal pine or balsam and breathe in its sweet aroma. The nomad with his tent on the back of his camel rejoices at the sight of an oasis where stately palms wave their plumes to heaven and give shade to the hot, weary traveler.

You who are nature lovers know the thrill of

pausing to listen to the music of the wind in the leaves. The soft murmur of the evergreens strikes a rich contrast to the sharp tinkle of a poplar's shapely hearts merrily fluttering in the breeze. How soothing are these sounds. Nature's music is balm for the soul.

Invariably when we think of home, a certain tree comes to mind. Somehow trees symbolize fundamental strengths we associate with places we hold dear. What tree do you prize?

A man and his daughter were walking one day in the forest behind their home. The little girl ran happily ahead, exclaiming as she went. "Do trees drink water, Daddy?" she queried. "Oh, yes," her father replied. "You know how sweet their water is when we make maple syrup in the springtime. You have tended the fire that boils down the first bucketfuls. You should know that trees drink water."

"Then why don't trees freeze up in winter," she asked, "like our pipe does that runs underground from the spring up there to our house?" She stopped and pointed up the hill through the pine trees to where a large springhouse stood. "That is a very good question," her father said. "Let me see if I can explain it to you. The tree is made up of cells where the water stays in warm weather. But before the cold weather comes, the tree withdraws the water and puts it into the spaces *between* the cells. Then, when the water freezes and increases in size, the empty cells act like little cushions. Nothing is torn or broken. The tree is spared destruction. Trees of the southland are spared this operation. They seem to know there should be no cold weather, so they do not prepare to freeze.

The child, silent for a moment, sighed, and said, "Then that man was right, Daddy, who said, 'Only God can make a tree!' "

The wisdom of our Creator is beautifully displayed all over the world. There is a kind of tree for every kind of situation—tall or small, stout or thin, for wet or dry climate, cold or hot. Almost every location on Earth has natural shelter provided by trees.

Trees fulfill one of the most important needs of humankind, and that is to supply fresh oxygen. We exhale poisonous carbon dioxide which trees use to nourish themselves, and they give us oxygen in return. This necessary recycling of air is called the carbon cycle. So we see that the Creator has a purpose for everything under the sun.

Often people chop down trees and allow the earth to wash away for lack of roots to hold it back. Thus, we see how trees play an important part in soil conservation. Trees need us, and we need trees to balance our life and our world.

Trees receive nourishment when food is drawn up through their roots and rootlets. Leaves act like little kitchens where water and mineral salts are "cooked" by the sun and made into sap for nourishing the whole tree. Chlorophyll then mixes with sap and undergoes a chemical reaction to provide sugar for the tree. Some sugar is changed into starch and stored to be used as the need arises.

You can discern quite well where a tree's roots and rootlets run beneath the earth if you see where the tree has arranged for its leaves to drop. When it rains, the leaves drop the water into the rootlet's mouth. And when the leaves drop in the fall, in four-season climates, they are sure to fall above the roots where their compost will renourish the mother plant. Nothing is wasted. Each act is planned for self-sustainment and the earth's nourishment.

In autumn, happy children, large and small, enjoy shuffling through dry leaves. It is estimated that a full-grown maple has enough leaves to cover at least a half acre if they are evenly spread. Little wonder rakers get weary!

Leaves are miraculous creations in themselves. Their upper portion is a thin, transparent membrane, much like our own skin. The underside of a leaf is coarser, deeper in color, and has larger veins. Beautiful leaf prints can be made by turning a leaf upside down, covering it with a white paper and drawing a crayon across its flat surface. Colors may be blended to resemble the natural color of an autumn leaf.

If you were to study the underside of a leaf under a microscope, you would be able to see tiny openings that resemble windows. The technical name for these is "stomata." An average leaf has up to one hundred thousand stomata per square inch. Each window has a tiny window shade which the intelligence of the tree opens during wet weather to invite moisture to enter, and closes in hot, dry weather to prevent undue evaporation.

Think of the divine wisdom behind each little window directing such a process, and then think of the numerous leaves on each tree. Then multiply this by the millions of trees in the world. You will begin to get a faint idea of the great intelligence constantly at work around us.

Despite the fact that this intelligence carefully tends each tiny window in every leaf to prevent moisture from escaping, a tree gives off much water to the atmosphere. For instance, an average oak probably gives off up to 180 gallons daily through the process of evaporation. Without this process, our air would be extremely dry and hardly tolerable.

Even as your thoughts and emotions are recorded

yearly in your physical body, so the tree contains a record of its lean years and its prosperous ones. Thus, nature provides a history book for us. When an old tree is sawed down, one can read the story of its life from its rings. Look carefully and you will see the past year on the outside circle and the year before that, closer to the center, and so on. Was it a healthy year for growing? Or were the leaves eaten severely by insects, or did they fall off because of drought? If the ring is fairly wide, this denotes well-being, if very narrow and scarred, it has recorded its struggles.

All natural life, whether a tree or a human being, leaves a report of its well-being in some way. The ancient trees of the western redwood forest tell a story of that part of the world before recorded history. The droughts, the storms, the hazards of fire and lightning are all recorded for posterity.

In people we can also notice the effects of attitudes that are positive, happy, and optimistic. Then observe the effects of the worrier, the fault-finder, the grudge bearer. All these attitudes are like historical marks, physically and mentally affecting an individual. How can we heal a wound? How can scar tissue be erased? By lifting our arms to God in prayer and with thankful hearts accepting His answers.

All trees have flowers, and some are more beautiful than others. What is lovelier than a jacaranda tree with its purple blooms outlined against a pale blue sky? Or the white dogwoods of Atlanta, a spectacle of singular beauty? Or the Japanese cherry trees that line the tidal basin in Washington, D.C., an attraction for visitors from all over the world? New England's apple blossom time is a time for lovers, but does not love paint blooms with nature's most beautiful of tints?

We can learn many lessons from trees. One valuable lesson is given by the white birch that graces New England's countryside. Storm and rain and heavy ice may come, but it gracefully bends low and lets the weather pass. In a nonresistant mood, it gives its all; and later, when the sun comes out and the storms cease, it sways, straightens up, and continues in its usual beauty. We, too, can learn to bend with the times, become nonresistant and endure hardships, and with much patience and love, survive. Life is for living, not for dying.

Our empathy for nature increases the more we learn about it. If we are part of a new race of man, what do you feel is our commission regarding the trees, animals, and things of nature? We are of common parentage, and all share a common lot.

"Do you have room for me in your life?" one leaf says to its neighbor. "Of course," replies the other leaf, and it moves over to share the sunshine. "Do you have room for me in your life?" says your neighbor. "Of course," you reply, "for the Lord has a purpose in our neighborliness, and the sooner we discover what it is, the sooner we will be blessed." Thus, every tree is most beautifully crowned, as each leaf finds its proper place and each bloom unfolds in season. The lessons of life are as blooms, and who among us would refuse a beautiful bouquet?

As we learn to grow like trees in ordered obedience to God's will and plan, the marks of Cain are replaced by the love of the Son of God. Forever He calls you from the depths of the beautiful forests to the edges of His shining lakes. "Come home," the Lord of nature sings. "Come home to me, the lighted One; come home to my smile and my beauty. Let my order ring sweet music in your ears, and let my peace bring tranquillity to your soul. Come home," He calls. "Come home!"

Snow

Security of a worldly nature is sought in sameness. A drive exists, especially with youth, to be like the next person, wear the same kind of jeans, copy hairstyles, eat the same foods, enjoy the same books, programs, and so on. This worldly attraction to sameness is partly responsible for some people being pulled into drug and sex abuse. People want to be on the same bandwagon in order to feel accepted and secure. Yet the Bible cautions: *"Therefore come out from them, and be separate from them, says the Lord."* (II Cor. 6:17)

Is there anything wrong with being different? The human fear of inadequacy would like to make us feel uncomfortable, yet as one views history, one can see that most outstanding leaders, most geniuses of our time, most advanced thinkers who have contributed to the upliftment of humankind were different from the run-of-the-mill person. They were different because they dared to be different. In fact, they were born with differences built in, we might say.

The humorous fact remains that, try as much as we will, we are *all* different. Try as hard as we may, we can never become exactly like someone else. Had God wanted us all to be the same, He would have made us puppets and put us on strings. But even in diversity there can be beautiful unity.

Nature repeats the story of humankind over and over. The tiny snowflake is probably the most perfect example of this. Of all the billions of snowflakes that fall each year, not one has ever been found to be identical to another. Each one is individual; each one is unique! This is a miracle in itself, to say nothing of the mystery behind each one's formation and beautiful effect.

There is a holiness and awesomeness that envelops almost anyone who steps out on a fresh snowfall. There is a spell of loveliness that grips one at that moment. Even the snow remover forgets his job as he is momentarily caught up in the glory of it. I have met many people who have never seen snow and may never see snow, and I feel that perhaps they have only half lived. Snow transports us into another world as mysterious as the quietness with which it falls. With each quiet snowfall a holy

communion is ushered in, as I have expressed in
the following poem:

Holy Communion

A world of white crept in last night,
  On padded wings it came in flight.
So softly did the snowflakes fall,
  I hardly knew they fell at all,
Until the sun its radiance lay
  Upon the Lord's filigree display.
The mounds on stonewall, fence, and post
  Remind one of the heavenly host.
I all but opened mouth to take
  Communion bread the Lord does break.

—Marjorie H. Russell

We have the record of the Lord inviting Job into
His inner world of peace when He asked Job:
"Have you entered the storehouses of the snow?"
(Job 38:22) The reply came: *"God thunders won-
drously with his voice; he does great things which
we cannot comprehend. For to the snow he says,
'Fall on the earth.'* " (Job 37:5, 6)

Snow has roused people's curiosity since early
times. They probably asked, "Why does the Creator give snow? Why can't we get all the moisture
we need at one time from rain and then survive the

cold without snow?'' The answer is obvious. If the amount of rain fell equal to the amount of snow, the summer would be a constant flood.

Again the question would arise, ''How is the snowflake made?'' Each flake forms around a central nucleus. The nucleus obviously has within it the divine plan already mapped out for each flake to follow as it evolves layer by layer.

Here is a lesson for us: the divine plan for you lies safely within you, ready for you to find and develop. Think of the great Mind that must have thought so carefully to create the billions of human beings who have trod the Earth, each one different from the other. The concept staggers the imagination! You have a unique role to play in this life, a role different from that of anyone else. It has been said that each of us has at least one double in this world. Yet even identical twins are different in some ways and have different missions to perform. This is a world filled with potential geniuses. The only problem lies in the fact that most people are not aware of their uniqueness to the extent that they capitalize on it for the glory of God.

As early as the 1500s, people began to study snowflakes. In fact, the Archbishop of Upsala, Olaus Magnus by name, wrote a book on the precious relics of natural phenomena. It contains a woodcut that was supposed to be a copy of one of the author's sketches. Three centuries later, in 1820, the Arctic explorer Scoresby made careful drawings of flakes he found while exploring the great North. Shortly thereafter in Japan, the lord of the castle of Koga, Toshitsua Doi, Ibaraki Prefecture, also made sketches of over 180 snow crystals that he observed through a microscope. His book was entitled "Sekka Zusetsu," meaning Illustrations of Snow Crystals. It was followed by a sequel, "Zoku Sekka Zusetsu."

In the late 1800s and early 1900s, Wilson A. Bentley of Jericho, Vermont, became interested in the exquisite forms of snowflakes. With the help of a photographic microscope that left nothing visible unrecorded, Bentley took over 6,000 snow and ice crystal pictures and placed them on record.

With all this close examination of the snowflake, however, scientists still did not understand how nature forms its flakes. In 1936 the late Professor Ukichiro Nakaya of Japan researched the formation of snow and succeeded in making artificial snow crystals so as to correlate their beauty with the formative conditions. Shortly after that, Vincent Schaefer of Schenectady, New York, created artificial snowflakes in a "cold box" into which he breathed. His moist breath condensed on a very cold rod in the cold box. Later he caused a snowfall by using dry ice. Finally, an x-ray specialist tried to coax the fragile beauties to reveal their innermost secrets of primary formation, and he accumulated many x-ray pictures that were of interest. With all this knowledge of crystalline water, however, there are still many details concerning the crystallography of ice and snow that remain unknown.

The size and shape of snowflakes depend upon temperature and the amount of moisture present. All flakes are hexagonal in shape, that is, six-sided. A crystal is structured in such a way that the molecules of water form an orderly structure in a hexagonal symmetry. When temperatures are high and the humidity is relatively great, the larger and more complex snow crystals usually occur in the front portion of a storm. Sometimes crystals have large, flat surfaces with intricate designs on them. These designs are indentations, ridges, grooves, and water films appearing in planned patterns as dots, dashes, ovals, triangles, lines, and so on.

Often the six-sided crystals have a central core, with spokes of wings, loops, and feathery decorations adhering to the spokes. The variety of design is almost unbelievable. The old-fashioned kaleidoscope is a dim facsimile of design variableness compared with nature's winter treat. Recently a process was developed in which a snowflake falls into a plastic solution, which quickly coats it. As the flake inside melts, it leaves the exact shape of the flake for decorative use.

If you were to step outdoors on a cold winter night with a small piece of black paper, you could catch some of the flakes. With the help of a flashlight and magnifying glass, you are in for a treat. Snowflakes are colorless and transparent, and they quickly melt. For this reason, many that you will view may not be perfect. They began perfect, but pressures, heat, or other conditions taking place during their fall damaged their perfect design.

Although snowflakes are transparent, we think of them as being white. The white color is due to the reflection of light by the tiny surfaces of the crystals. Black snow is black because of dust particles in it. In Greenland snow sometimes falls as red snow or green snow. This is due to tiny living organisms in the snow that are too minute to be obvious to the naked eye.

Have you ever hiked up a mountain and come to the snow line? From there you had to use a different method of hiking, perhaps by donning snowshoes or skis. Snow lies on the tops of most high mountains all summer, even in the hottest countries. The height of the sun, winds, temperature, and moisture contribute to the height of the snow line. The snow line in the Rocky Mountains is about two miles above sea level. The snow line is about three miles above sea level in the tropics, whereas in the Alps, it is only a mile and two-thirds above sea level. The snow line in Greenland is a half mile above sea level, and in polar regions it is at sea level.

Of course, the tree line, as well as the fauna and flora, are also affected by the snow. It is interesting to hike up Mt. Washington in New Hampshire and notice the change in flower growth where the snow lingers until midsummer. Alpine flowers are quite tiny and of a different variety than their cousins that grow in the lowlands. Some trees, when measured in summer when the snow has gone, are only a few feet high, although they may be 80 to 100 years old.

Snow crystals vary in shape, although they, like snow crystals, are always six-sided. The most unusual is the dendrite shape; then there are the needle, bullet, column-shaped, and columns which are capped at one or both ends with plates. The hexagonal columns are three-to-five times longer than they are thick. Some resemble spools that thread comes on, others are like ornate cuff links with intricate designs. Perhaps the rarest of all ice crystal formations is the pyramidal, especially the double pyramidal, which is two pyramidal ends base to base, with or without a section of a column between them. These dainty forms are so tiny and fragile that we might call them Mother Nature's sparkling display of jewels.

Perhaps you have looked at the full moon and seen a beautiful halo around it. Have you ever wondered what causes this? The lovely rainbow rings are caused by the moonlight passing uninterruptedly through the ice crystals from one hexagonal face to the second one beyond it, that is, in-and-out faces inclined to each other at an angle of sixty degrees in the case of the most common twenty-two-degree halo. It is difficult to imagine how our Creator can line up minute crystals in such a fashion.

When winter comes, we never think of flowers, but there *are* flowers present. They are called ice flowers. Have you ever found flowers formed on the surface of ice? If not, you may want to search for some next winter. Small flowers appear as if embroidered into a fabric, only the fabric is a sheet of ice, and the flowers are also ice. This is due to the molecular action going on within the water as it freezes. What a marvelous Creator we have!

Some of the loveliest and perhaps the most delicate designs may be found in frost. Take time to walk outdoors on a cool, frosty fall morning and observe with care the lovely crystals clinging to tall grasses or frozen leaves. Frost on windowpanes makes us feel we are looking into a dense forest or peering deep into an ocean of unknown form and beauty. Ostrich feathers, Christmas trees, fish, ferns, mosses, and flocks of birds appear in full array, each a pure gem of precious delicacy, forming a jewel design that defies the finest imagination for elegance.

If you have visited northern states in the wintertime, you may have witnessed the occasional occurrence of hoarfrost. This happens when the humidity is very high and a sudden cold snap occurs. Trees, especially along the river's edge, become laden with long, fringed crystals. The covering is so complete that entire trees are transformed into crystal trees. The effect is unworldly. Apparently there are places in the Holy Land that have hoarfrost, because it is mentioned in Psalms. *Praise the Lord, O Jerusalem! Praise your God . . . He gives snow like wool; he scatters hoarfrost like ashes. He casts forth his ice like morsels; who can stand before his cold?* (Psalms 147: 12, 16, 17)

Winter, with its snow, ice, and purity has beauty and appeal to those who live in northern climates. Northern children love nothing better than to go out in the snow and dig caves for playhouses or build igloos of the sticky snow that occurs when the sun comes out. I recall our children building a cave of several adjoining rooms where they played happily for many days. Snow can provide much entertainment in this way, along with cross-country skiing, snowshoeing, bobsledding, and just plain sliding down a snowdrift on the seat of one's snowsuit. People of the North dress for the cold and enjoy the climate.

Perhaps you can remember the day of ice houses. These were large shacks where blocks of ice, sawed from a nearby lake, were stacked and stored under a deep blanket of sawdust for summer use. Even today young and old enjoy munching on a chunk of ice when the day is hot!

Winter carnivals are held in many of the northern states, as well as northern countries around the world. Japan, with a total space of somewhat more than 14,000 miles, consists of a number of islands which form a bow-shaped archipelago. Its climate varies from subtropical to subarctic. The northern half of the main island of Honshu receives snowfalls often from three to ten feet deep. An annual Sapporo Snow Festival in Hokkaido features statues made from powdered snow and water. Driving through our little town in New Hampshire at our carnival time, one may see snow sculptures on display in front of public buildings, schools, or on expansive lawns of estates.

Sleigh rides are also being reinstated as a social custom. As the old tune says: "What fun it is to ride in a one-horse open sleigh!" There truly is no thrill quite like a sleigh ride on a quiet moonlit night. The light of the moon glistens on a crystalline world, and all that can be heard is the dull thud of horses' hooves as the sleigh runners glide over a padded road. Clean, fresh air fills our lungs and stings our cheeks as we nestle snugly beneath a layer of blankets.

Many great poets have been inspired by the beauty of the snow and have written at length about it. William Cullen Bryant was one of them:

Snow

Here delicate snow-stars, out of the cloud,
   Come floating downward in airy play,
Like spangles dropped from the glistening crowd
   That whiten by night the Milky Way.

Ants

In Proverbs we read: *Go to the ant, O sluggard; consider her ways, and be wise. Without having any chief, officer or ruler, she prepares her food in summer, and gathers her sustenance in harvest.* (Prov. 6:6-8) Industry and cooperation are the tools of success for any individual or society, especially when the industry and cooperation are based upon love, free will, and a Godly plan. From our study of ants, it appears that their colonies succeed by following such principles. There is great loyalty displayed to the point of one worker's laying down its life for the sake of others; there is great diligence exercised and much ingenuity displayed in their maneuvers.

For instance, an ant hauling a crust of bread to its hill is carrying a load probably seventy times its own weight. We may ask where its energy to carry such loads comes from. If a human being lifts an object twice his own weight, he feels quite efficient. But there is the human concept connected with work that says one must eat so much food in order to generate enough energy to work. How does an ant receive enough nourishment from a few drops of liquid a day to perform such tiring tasks? There must be an unseen energy flowing from our spiritual source that humans and all related life inherit.

It was Benjamin Franklin, himself an example of industry and cooperation, who observed early in life that sloth makes things difficult, but industry makes them easy; and he that riseth late must trot all day and shall scarcely overtake his business at night; while laziness travels so slowly that poverty soon overtakes him. Certainly this accusation cannot be leveled at the ant. The ant is an early riser and is quickly about its Father's business. From dawn to nightfall it appears very aware of its responsibilities in connection with the rest of the members of its society, being diligent to do all things it must do, to its level best.

What a wonderful human society we would have if we decided to do the same. It has often been said that if every person calling himself a Christian would exemplify the principles laid down by our Master, the world could be drastically improved overnight! And it is a fact that as everyone lives up to the highest ideal he perceives, regardless of religious belief, the world will be a better place in which to live. Cooperation and industry begin with the individual and is shared in the family, then moves into the world.

There is not a realtor or insurance agent who will not ask: "Do you own your own home?" If the answer is yes, a whole range of personal involvement is felt. After all, there is no place like home! Yet, how would you feel if some huge giant decided to step on your house and squash your family under his foot? This is not a pleasant thought. Likewise we need to be more respectful of the labors of the tiny ant as he builds the place he feels is his home.

To an ant, a june bug would appear as large as an elephant, and a caterpillar would seem to be some threatening monster. Yet the fearless little ant proceeds on its way, undaunted by seeming outer threats. I have never heard anyone pleading the courage of an ant, but it might be something to think about. This is especially true when problems tend to loom larger than they really are. Perhaps we should change that popular saying to, "Don't make a mountain out of an anthill."

Amazingly enough, there are over 8,000 different kinds of ants. Did you know there are shepherd ants who gather tiny aphid bugs and pasture them on milkweed plants? There are farmer ants who grow their own vegetables underground. There are carpenter ants who gnaw tunnels in wood and are destructive. And in warmer climates there are slave-making ants who kidnap children from other ant nations and make them do their work. In Africa there are military ants who make war on every living creature in their path. Even elephants, zebras, giraffes, and tigers flee from them, for they know they will be eaten alive if they do not. And there are many other nations of ants as well.

We are all well-acquainted with the ants that get into our pantries and find an open honey pot. They love sweets as much as we do, so we cannot blame them. Obviously, we can be wise and remove temptation from them by keeping our food tightly sealed and stored.

Ants make their homes in many places. Probably the anthill is the most noticeable one to us; but stones, wood, paper, or leaves are also used for homes.

In an anthill we find three types of ants—the queen, the royalty, and the workers. Among the workers are nurses that tend the baby ants, and the queen, scouts, guards, and warriors to protect the community home, food gatherers, housekeepers who clear the rooms and tunnels, and so on. Each ant is either born knowing what its job is or is told by the queen that rules the colony.

The queen may live as long as fifteen years, performing her role of loving obedience to the Creator's plan for the continuance of community life. She sets the example for the entire population. When she dies, they all die, for without the queen, those in the colony lose their desire to live.

The queen is larger in form than the rest, and she lays all the eggs for the community. Devoted nurses wash her continually with their tongues, keeping her spotlessly clean and shiny. They carry her eggs to other rooms, and when the young appear, they feed them, moving them from room to room as they need more air or moisture or warmth. The devotion of the nurses leaves nothing to be desired. They live to give their all, and give, they do!

Among those born to the queen, we find new workers, new princes, and princesses, who in turn will become queens of new colonies. Princes and princesses have wings and better eyes than workers. In spring they have matured, and on an appointed day known only to ants, the royal princes and princesses fly off on gossamer wings and mate in the skies. What a wonder this complex procedure is, and with what skill it seems to be performed.

The act of procreation is carried on in ecstatic joy. After this, the mated princess, who is now a queen, descends to the earth, while the princes die because they are too lazy to feed themselves. The queen's part thus completed, she obediently bites off her pretty wings and goes into seclusion, hiding away under an old log or rock, sometimes for a year or more.

In this state of semi-hibernation she receives no food. She lays her eggs and feeds the worm-like babies that hatch from her eggs with the oily spittle from her mouth. Soon the babies spin silky cocoons and remain in these homemade cradles for several weeks.

When the queen mother helps them out, they are not plump, pretty babies, but are runty, under-fed little ants, clamoring for food. At that, Mother then breaks the seal she has placed on her door and forages for food for herself and her babies. As the young ones increase in size and strength, their roles in the new colony are clear-cut. Some workers then become food gatherers and bring it to the royalty. Others begin to construct a new anthill with tunnels, apartments, and rooms on main and side streets.

We can see what a catastrophe it would be if a queen became an egotistical despot, abusing her workers and enslaving her children instead of allowing them to take their appointed places in the overall plan of action for a new community.

Ordered goodwill is the foundation of all successful endeavor.

An ant worker is equipped with two stomachs for carrying food. One is for her own food, and the other is to carry food back home to the queen, babies, and other workers. At home, the food gatherer places her mouth against the nurse's mouth to transfer the food. The nurse keeps some for herself and then gives some of her drop of nourishment to the babies or to the queen. This is how the whole colony is fed.

When one ant wants food from a worker, it taps gently on the other's head with its feelers, using their telegraph code. They seem to talk this way, and they talk a lot. Watch and see how problems are solved by this tap-talking process with feelers.

Workers sometimes need help to drag home a heavy prize. If a dead caterpillar is found near an anthill, the guards go inside the hill to report their find. Then the workers will come out and examine it. Next, they will begin to divide the food into segments small enough for an ant to tote into the hill for later consumption. The teamwork on such a project is ordered and efficient.

It is interesting to observe the personal responsibility accepted without question by those of strong jaws who stand guard outside the doors of the anthill to fight off intruders, and those obliging workers who willingly carry out rubbish to the ant dump, some distance from the hill. There is no weekly rubbish collector that comes by; the work is done very efficiently every day by the workers, who do not allow debris to accumulate.

This presents a striking parallel to those human beings who watchfully clean out the tempting rubbish from their thinking each day before retiring. It was Ignatius of Loyola who used Aristotelian propositions of seven parallel lines, one line for each day. On the day's line he would place a dot for every sin he was aware of and desired to clean out from his experience.

The ant guards that keep watch over the hill permit no unwanted strangers to enter. If they are not of their nation, they are chased off. Occasionally a stranger approaches, thinking, "Ah, here is a nice house where I can move in and take my ease." But the guard is not sleeping. With firm determination he turns the other away. If we were as adamant about negative thoughts and temptations, we would soon be free from many illnesses, both mental and physical. If self-discipline works so well for an ant, how much more should it work for us.

If an ant had a Bible, I am sure the words of the Psalmist would be in it: *Create in me a clean heart, O God, and put a new and right spirit within me. . . . Restore to me the joy of thy salvation,*

118

and uphold me with a willing spirit. (Psalms 51:10, 12)

If things go wrong, an ant calls for help and immediately sets to work to correct the situation. Humanity can learn a lesson from this, instead of sitting idly by, blaming someone else. Indifference to repairing damage is not tolerated in the anthill. Things out of order must be taken care of immediately. Order is heaven's first law, and we are slowly learning this lesson the ant learned long ago. The humble ant knows what the result of self-concern and indulgence is, and will have no part in it.

An example of this is the story of the ancient city of Sybaris. Founded in 720 B.C. in the foot of Italy, it flourished as a green bay tree in its licentiousness. Immorality and self-indulgence prevailed in its population of over 300,000, so that for all its worldly grandeur and power, it fell to the small city of Croton. Pythagoras recorded the event. Sybaris was so completely overwhelmed, it soon vanished and was forgotten. So completely forgotten, in fact, modern archaeologists have hardly found a trace of it. How important it is that we take a regular time to turn within, to bring ourselves into order, and to connect with our quiet center of God, where we cannot be pushed off our divine base.

In regard to ants, an amusing situation occurred

one day when my father took my mother, who was then single, for a walk. It was a beautiful day, and my daddy, who lived at the time in the city, was enjoying the countryside. His heart was full to overflowing with love for my mother, and he was confused, as most young men probably are, about just how to best express it. As they walked along he finally became exasperated at his overwhelming desire to make her his own. He sat her down on a small mound and proposed to her. The mound turned out to be an anthill! Needless to say, it was an exciting day for Mother in more ways than one.

Ants have brains, mouths, eyes, jaws which move from side to side, two noses in the form of feelers, and six legs. Only the royalty have wings. What wisdom has decreed this order!

The ant shines its armor often with its oily saliva. It breathes through two rows of holes in its sides, for it has no lungs. Tubes carry air to all parts of its body. The ant has combs on each side of its two forelegs which are used to dust off its body. Its heart lies behind a big nerve that runs down its underside. Ears have never been found in an ant, but through experiments we know they have some way of hearing. Perhaps the antennae have a triple purpose—to see, smell, and hear.

We are often told we should live balanced lives. Yet, as we view the life of an ant, it would seem that this law of nature is broken. Surprisingly enough, however, all work and no play even makes Johnny Ant a very dull ant, and he is smart enough to know this! Ants take time out to play. They roll on the ground and wrestle with each other, working their ant muscles. They even play ball with a grain of wheat or grass seed!

It is also known that the ant colonies have mass meetings in their underground halls. They sit quietly listening by gently waving their feelers to and fro. Are their feelers portable radios? What are their meetings about? The mystery of ant conventions is still an unanswered riddle. Perhaps it has something to do with the governing of their ant colony. In any event, there are no riots, and all is accomplished with goodwill as they leave the meeting. Man, who is busy conquering space travel, needs to learn more about the good Earth upon which he is planted and how to live as harmoniously as these small insects.

Ants form into nations. There may be a number of cities in one field comprising several different ant nations. Several cities may belong to one nation, if the queens are sisters. Ants distinguish between relatives and strangers by their sense of smell. Those of the same nation smell alike. There is usually no trespassing, for scouts patrol the borders. Trespassers are punished and sometimes beaten up!

If an attack is threatened by foreign ants, the guards run home with the news. There is no time for use of feelers. They bang their heads against the walls of their tunnels like striking a fire bell. In this way everyone knows the battle is about to begin, and everyone rallies to the fight. An ant will die to save the lives of the members of his community.

One of the most interesting nations of ants that have undergone a lot of study is the harvester ant. These ants are very fond of Aristida grass seed and have a highly developed ant civilization. Workers who are sent out into the field climb up the grass and cut off the seed head, which is passed to another worker who carries it to ant city. At the city entrance, which has been cleared and smoothed, the receiving workers clean off the husks from each grain and pass them to other workers who carry the grains into the rooms below. There the miller takes the grain and with strong jaws grinds it into flour. Spittle is mixed with the four, which is then rolled up into dough balls that are carried out to be baked in the sun. As soon as they are thoroughly baked, they are stored for later eating. The intelligence of such a procedure is truly amazing!

Earlier I spoke about the farmer ants. These are ants that live on home-raised food. Their entire consumption is mushrooms that are raised in tiny mushroom cellars. Some farmer ant cities may be as large as half of one of our city blocks and may be eighteen feet under the earth.

Somehow the tiny ants know their mushrooms must be fertilized in order to grow. They make fertilizer out of leaves, thoroughly chewed and combined with saliva. The fertilizer is then stuck to either the floor or ceiling of the room where the mushrooms are planted. Tirelessly, the ant workers weed their gardens, pulling out the foreign mushrooms that spring up, and a pruning process sets in until the plant produces the succulent portions valued for eating. It staggers the imagination to realize the number of mushrooms needed to feed enough ants covering half a city block.

Orange growers find these ants a problem, since orange leaves are often chosen for fertilizing purposes. A whole tree can be quickly stripped, as ant after ant departs with a leaf parasol in its mouth.

The tree ants of Africa and Indo-Australia make nests in trees inside leaves fastened together by silk. For many years people wondered where these ants got the silk to fasten the living leaves together, since there was no known source of silk available in those parts. After patient observation, naturalists discovered that the ants were using their own larvae to produce the cement-silk needed. At pupating age, the larvae would normally spin cocoons about themselves. The silk they manufactured from their own bodies was a liquid. The ant workers found that they could pick up a larva, and by squeezing it very carefully, as you would a tube of household cement, they could stick together the edges of two leaves. Carefully the workers held the leaves in place until the silk cement was hardened and a beautiful, waterproof, camouflaged nest was ready for occupancy. From then on it was a matter of minutes before the whole tribe moved in and made themselves at home in the treetops of an African jungle forest. With a brain the size of two pinheads, the ant certainly does very well!

It was Aristotle who said that compulsion is contrary to nature. Obviously, the ant does not work under compulsion or its work would prove unsuccessful. There is a beautiful harmony of purpose expressed through the intelligence of such living beings.

The next time you come across an anthill, pause for a while and see what is going on. Those of us who appreciate ants will come into possession of some of nature's most precious secrets.

Animals

It was Frank Buck who "brought them back alive." He went on safaris in Africa and captured wild animals, caged them, shipped them to the United States, and sold them for large sums of money. Most of these unlucky animals ended up in zoos or circuses. Since the Earth teems with over three million different kinds of animals, we realize Buck scarcely made a dent in the animal population that has proliferated since the day Noah very carefully, at the Lord's command, took the animals two by two into the Ark for safekeeping. The names of the animals were not listed by Noah, but numerous references are made throughout the Bible to various kinds of animals. The lion that David faced and killed barehanded was apparently not that rare, nor was the fox, wildcat, or other animals which are harmful to sheep.

In Exodus we read that horses were used by Pharaoh to draw his chariots of war. When God led the Hebrews through the Red Sea: *The Egyptians pursued, and went in after them into the midst of the sea, all Pharaoh's horses, his chariots, and his horsemen. . . . and the Lord routed the Egyptians in the midst of the sea.* (Exod. 14:23, 27) *"I will sing to the Lord, for he has triumphed gloriously; the horse and his rider he has thrown into the sea."* (Exod. 15:1) King David likewise had large quantities of horses enlisted in his cavalry. In those days horses were unshod, and those with hard hooves were especially prized. Solomon had horses and chariots in abundance. He found that the horse provided great assistance in the maintenance of his vast empire. Later, II Kings mentions a trade of some 2,000 horses the king of Assyria wanted to make with Israel at the time of Hezekiah. (II Kings 18:23) That was some "horse trading," as the saying goes!

The prophets Isaiah, Jeremiah, Ezekiel, Hosea, Joel, Amos, Micah, Habakkuk, Haggai, Zechariah, and John the Revelator mention horses as symbols and as tools of either victory or defeat. The Lord made plain through Hosea that He would be the saving grace of Judah and that they were not to put their saving trust in horses or wealth. *"I will have pity on the house of Judah, and I will deliver them by the Lord their God; I will not deliver them by bow, nor by sword, nor by war, nor by horses, nor by horsemen.''* (Hos. 1:7)

This did not mean the people were not to build a good defense in the outer. The Lord knew they needed outer measures of defense, but He wanted them to give their full attention to Him so that He could direct their actions for successful warfare. This still holds true today.

We have been given dominion over our lives and affairs, but we are to look to God first as to how to use the physical tools He has given us for successful, happy, safe living. Foolish indeed is the person who throws away his hoe and rake and expects God to grow his garden. Just as we are co-workers with God, animals are co-workers with us. Humbly they do our bidding, and because of this, the land is blessed.

Animals live in all places on the Earth, from the high mountains to the woodlands, swamps, fields, parched prairies, bleak deserts, tangled jungles and, yes, even in the waters. When we use the term *animal,* we immediately think of recognizable creatures with backbones, walking the Earth. We forget that some animals are so small they are microscopic. Some one-celled creatures are so hard to define that scientists cannot decide if they should be called plants or animals. Animals eat plants or other animals, while plants usually get their food from air and soil. However, there are some exceptions to this. The sundew and pitcher plants, as well as a few others, live on insects trapped by their leaves, which act as clutching hands. Plants on the whole are stationary, while animals can move around. Although sponges and sea lilies may look like plants, they are really animals.

Whereas the one-celled animal is probably the smallest animal, the largest animal known today is most likely the one-hundred-ton blue whale. Even the giant dinosaurs that lived in the age of the reptiles were not as large as the whales of today. Whereas a land animal's body or a bird's body is limited by the amount of air that will support it, a whale's body is supported by water and keeps on growing and growing.

It is not evident why whales left the land and decided to make the sea their home. Evidence shows the bones that were left from the four legs whales once walked on when they were land creatures. Whales give birth to live babies and nurse them with milk, as do land mammals. Interestingly enough, their milk looks and tastes much like cow's milk. A baby whale is about the size of two elephants.

A whale has nostrils on the top of its head or the

tip of its snout. These nostrils are a blowhole through which the whale breathes, for he does not seem to have a sense of smell.

As you may recall, it was Jonah who was reported to have lived in the belly of a whale. According to reports of naturalists, a whale's stomach is like an apartment house. It has as many as five or six compartmented rooms. One can imagine rebellious Jonah sitting amidst the seaweed and dead fish that floated through the various chambers, and the mess he must have been when he was cast out and walked into the city of Nineveh. Doubtless, people stopped whatever they were doing and gave him their undivided attention, for more reasons than one!

In the late '50s, two whales ventured up the Penobscot River into the large pool at Bangor. They romped and played daily before an admiring crowd that came from miles around to see the spectacle. Lovers and old married couples, mothers with children, wayfarers, traveling salesmen, businessmen on their way to work, and dozens of others grew into large crowds. A traffic policeman was sent to handle traffic. Newspapers picked up the story.

After an exciting week or two, several people decided to harpoon the whales. They got into a small boat, to the dismay of the crowds. Hastily letters and editorials were printed, and legal pressure was put on them to stop. However, they were determined to kill, and out they went to attack the friendly creatures.

The whales quickly picked up the message. They sought cover of the deeper water. As the boat approached, they gave a sudden flick of the tail, and over went the men, with knives, harpoons, spears, and other elements of slaughter, headfirst into the water. The crowd cheered! By the time a new crew had been rallied, the law was upon them, and the whales safely left for happier places at sea. We pray that the time will come when man can view the joys of earth life without thought of destruction in his mind and heart. *The earth is the Lord's, and the fullness thereof, the world and those who dwell therein; for he has founded it upon the seas, and established it upon the rivers.* (Psalms 24:1, 2)

Animals seem to be able to adapt to almost any spot on Earth; however, no one animal is able to live in all places. The same kinds of animals can usually be found in similar environments, although there are sometimes strays with odd habits that defy naturalists.

Most animals have fur that blends naturally with their surroundings. When winter comes, many northern animals change to white or a lighter color so as not to be easily seen by predators. Wolves, foxes, hares, and bears are some of these.

Although many animals have horns or claws, teeth, chemical deterrents, or lashing tails, their biggest protection is by flight. All but a few of the slowpokes, like the turtle who withdraws into its shell, and the porcupine who ambles along, relying on his full stack of quills, either take to the bush or run for their lives.

One year as winter approached, I went down into the cellar of a house we had just bought and was horrified to find that a porcupine had also moved in. The cellar window had been left open, and he had climbed in! Making a hasty retreat to the top of the stairs, I paused long enough to inform him, lovingly but firmly, that he was entirely out of place living in our house and that he must leave immediately. I told him of all the nice places the Lord had provided outside.

I gave him a week or two, and when I went down to the cellar again, he was gone. A few of his quills had dropped, which I cleaned up, but other than that he had politely left.

We need to remember that God's intelligence is in His creatures. It may not be in the English or French language, but I am sure the intent of the mind and heart is sent out to the creature and the message is received. Through our Jesus Christ power, we have dominion over the Earth.

You may never tangle with a porcupine, but

your dog may. In this event, I trust you do not have the problem we had in northern Maine when our dog ran into our yard with a face full of porcupine quills. Quills sink quickly into the body, and if not pulled out immediately, they work into the bloodstream and kill the animal. It is good to understand that each quill is a tiny barb somewhat like a fishhook. The more you pull, the more flesh the hook grabs. Pliers are needed for such an operation. It was a painful ordeal for our pet, but we succeeded in extracting all the quills before they disappeared. One could see them sinking in swiftly.

What we did not know then, but know now, may save you or your pet a painful hour of quill extraction. We have been told there is a hydraulic type of propulsion within each quill that causes it to work into an object. One will work right through your shoe if you step on it. They are very strong and sharp, and children should never play with them. The trick is to use scissors and cut a small portion off the end of the quill. This releases the hydraulic pressure and the quill may be drawn out of the flesh with little damage.

One of nature's curious animals is the Scandinavian lemming. Their bodies are small, four or five inches long, and they are brownish-yellow with dark spots. Being cousins of the mouse, they live much the same as most rodents. But at regular intervals, once every five years or so, hordes of the small creatures begin to march out of their homes into the mountains.

They march like an unruly army across fields, woods, walls, streams, and mountains until they reach the Atlantic Ocean. They raid places on the way, and people are in horror of their coming, since nothing seems to stop them. This has been going on since lemmings came into existence. Many of them die from hunger, fatigue, or disease on the long trip to the sea. They go either west toward the Atlantic or east toward the Gulf of Bothnia.

When they arrive at the water, their leaders enter the deep, and the rest of the countless hordes of animals follow until all are drowned. This strange behavior has baffled naturalists, since these are the only creatures on Earth that do such a thing. What sponsors this death march? What purpose is performed by it? And how do the creatures know the exact time to go on it? There is obviously much going on in the line of communication in animals that we know little about.

A theory has been suggested by some that the animals are overpopulated and go to deliberate extinction. Or that they become hungry and march out in search of food, and when they come to the ocean, they do not realize that it is not just another stream they can cross. None of these theories answers the question as to why they set out at a certain time, and why some go and others are left behind.

The courtship of some animals is intriguing to observe. It is true that "it's love that makes the world go round." We see pictures of monkeys kissing, zebras nestling together, giraffes bumping heads, and rhinoceroses snuggled head-to-head in blissful oneness. Elephants entwine trunks in loving embrace, and foxes do a fox-trot with each other. And in case you wondered where the term *bear hug* came from, it originated with the bears. They actually hug and kiss as they mate. The frog whistles, trills, and calls its mate, who only responds to the right species. The procedure is elaborate or simple, but the goal is the same—love and reproduction of the species.

Most courtships have definite steps and stages. If a certain step or stage is missing, the animal does not respond. Each animal is born knowing instinctively what the right mating practice is. Courtship, then, becomes an insurance policy against mixed breeds.

Squirrels have an interesting pattern of courtship. Signals between the sexes are given by waving the tail during a mating chase. With gray squirrels, the male yearling and adult give short, rapid, fore-and-aft flips, and then feed the female. Other squirrels have either a slow waving of the tail or a circular waving, depending on the species. The female gives chase and then lets the male catch her. In most cases the male takes the lead in courtship.

Squirrels are also known to perform some amusing tricks. A friend reported watching a squirrel play happily with a rabbit in her backyard. There was a row of cement blocks that bordered her driveway. The rabbit crouched down beside a block. Then the squirrel climbed up on the block and leaped over her onto the grass beyond. It would then return to the cement block and jump over her again. When they had enough of doing that, they romped around the lawn, chasing each other by turn and then returned to play with the cement block again.

Another friend reported an incident regarding her bird feeder. The feeder was suspended on a rod from a tree limb, but when a squirrel shimmied down the rod and easily got the birdseed, she decided to remove the rod and suspend the feeder by a string. The next day she looked out and there was the squirrel, hanging upside down from the limb, toes firmly dug in, and pulling up, hand over hand, the rope with the bird feeder attached. When the feeder was in his front paws, he shook off the seed, then quickly scampered down to the ground to eat it. Such acts surpass instinct and certainly indicate that reasoning is taking place.

No doubt you have many stories you could add to the interesting tales about squirrels. I have one about a squirrel and a chipmunk. We have in our arboretum a beautiful Bartlett pear tree, which last year was full of young pears just beginning to ripen. A large squirrel was watching and waiting, and when the pears got almost ready for picking, he got there first. He not only picked one, but many were dropped. He ran down and took one bite out of each and ran off. The next day he reappeared to create more damage.

In the meantime, there was a tiny chipmunk who also visited our tree. He was a frugal little creature. He would bite off one pear and then chase down the tree and devour it in its entirety. We did not mind sharing with Chippie, but we decided to put a stop to the ravaging the squirrel was doing to our pear tree. Around the tree, above a hollow in the trunk which the chipmunk had been using as his route up the tree, we placed a collar of wire that stood straight out. The squirrel was put out of business, and the fruit continued to ripen until the day of harvest.

We were removing the wire collar when down the tree little Chippie came. He slid deliberately under the collar as if to show off that he could do it, then he came to a halt. While we stood and watched, he glared at us, as if to say, "How dare you try to keep us out!" Our gardener is still laughing.

City dwellers reported watching a gray squirrel stash nuts in a hole in a tree in front of their windows. When winter came, each good day he would take two nuts out on a horizontal limb, eat them and then lie down on his belly, spread his bushy tail up over his back like a blanket, and snooze in the sun. There is nothing like a picnic in the park, even for a squirrel.

Much is written about red foxes, as they seem to have endearing ways in their family life. The male and female are devoted to one another and are believed to be mated for life. The intelligent rearing of the pups shows an advanced development of love in the animal kingdom. Both parents help establish a nursery den, and both have a hand in training and feeding their offspring.

Midwinter is the foxes' mating time. After mating, the couple travel for some time looking for the most suitable home. They often find an old woodchuck hole or an abandoned burrow that they can enlarge to suit their purposes. They usually have two or three backup dens just in case of emergency.

There are usually four to eight pups born in early spring. They are loving and playful, and the vixen tolerates their playful mauling with patience, while papa brings them a mouse or a rabbit for supper. The mother eats the offering first and then regurgitates it for the young to eat.

Although papa does not live in the den with mama and his little foxes, he is close by to guard them, and his warning bark is heeded at the first sign of danger. If a dog finds the den, it is possible for papa and mama to quietly and quickly move their little family out the back door to one of their alternative homes. If the roof leaks or the snow gets too deep, the family again moves to another country home. Their dens are not too far underground, for foxes love the sunlight.

The parents allow the little foxes to play with toy sticks, wing feathers, or bones inside the den. If the safety of the family is threatened and the family must move to another home, papa picks up the tiny pups by the back of the neck with his mouth and carefully carries them. The children's playthings are also taken when the family moves.

Such tender, loving care and family faithfulness cannot go unnoticed. When the pups grow up they express the same virtues as did their parents. It is only a matter of ten weeks before the pups are on their way to a life of their own. By then, they have had an opportunity to explore the nearby terrain, and at summer's end they leave for good, and a new family circle begins.

Some people enjoy taming wild animals and keeping them in their homes as pets. This may or may not be the best thing to do. Most mammals that come into human possession do so because they are injured or sick. Few young animals are really deserted, although it may appear so. Sometimes the mother leaves a fawn unattended for hours to allow it freedom, although she watches carefully from a nearby thicket. Mother rabbits often feed their young at dawn and then leave for the day. People who come across these young ones tend to believe they have been forsaken.

Some animals, squirrels, for instance, transmit diseases to people by fleas or ticks. Extreme caution should be exercised in handling wild creatures until they have been bathed and dusted with flea powder used for cats or dogs.

Many wild animals, though cute and tame as babies, become tough and difficult as they mature to adulthood and are ready to mate. Their behavior is not always understood by humans and can result in tragedies of one kind or another.

If the adult animal is released after growing up domestically, it may be killed by cats or dogs or humans, because it fears no human. Or it may end up raiding garbage cans or biting children who play with it. Then, too, it does not understand who its natural predators are and can be quickly seized and killed.

If you take a wild animal when it is young and have an enjoyable experience raising it, you will want to keep it through its mature years, because, unfortunately, we humans become attached to animals. There is the possibility at this point of legal difficulties, because most governments require certain permits which are difficult to obtain. In short, it is best to leave wild animals that appear to be healthy, although unattended, in their natural habitat. If a leg or wing or body is broken, or if some aid of a temporary nature can be given to enable a wild animal to continue in its wild state, then it is well and good to help it. But let us not become overly sentimental. It does wildlife little good, and there are more acceptable channels of expression for one's emotions.

I once went into a drugstore on a summer day and sat down on a stool for a cool drink. Soon a man and woman came in with a lynx on a chain. They sat the lynx on the stool next to me, and we all chatted pleasantly, the lynx eyeing every movement around it. It seems this was a so-called abandoned animal the man had come across while mountain climbing, which he brought home and tamed. Later on, the animal became unmanageable. After a series of clawing events, they let it go. The unfortunate thing was that it had not learned to hunt proper food, and it had no can opener to use. We can only wish such animals good luck and God's blessing.

A scene of elephant love was pictured in the newspaper not long ago. There was an elephant holding trunks with another elephant which was dying. The article told about five elephants that had been captured in Africa and brought to Germany for circus use. They had displayed tremendous loyalty to each other over the years. Now Mani was sick and dying, and her grieving friends kept a vigil over her. The four healthy elephants stood by their sick friend, supporting her so she would not fall down in her weakness. Each of them would take turns gently caressing her, running their trunks over her ears and over her back and legs. If elephants could cry, we are certain they were doing so.

As you probably know, elephants are faithful to their mates and to one another. One buck often has as many as three wives, but he is loyal to all of them. When a mother elephant gives birth, midwives stand by her to attend the delivery. If a small calf is in danger, the mother will risk her life to rescue it. If a hunter wounds an adult elephant, four others have been seen to come and pick it up in their trunks and carry it to safety. When an elephant dies, they all express loving concern by standing for a while in silence. Then they get branches or earth and cover the body.

We have spoken about animal homes. Although some animals do not have a regular home, they do claim a certain territory as their own. Some areas are large, and others are small, but each area is judged by the animal as being able to support it with enough food and pasturage and safe hiding places. For instance, a rabbit family will usually be satisfied with an eight-acre territory, whereas a mountain lion has need of a great deal of territory, even up to fifty miles.

Even as homes vary for animals, so does child care. Some animals forsake their young at birth; others are tender and caring parents. The males usually leave most of the rearing to the female. This is true of the black bear, so prolific in western United States national parks.

When born, the black bear cub is blind and covered with soft baby hair that is black. The cubs are amusing as they cuff one another and grow into knowing what is right to do and what is a no-no. They soon have much practice in tree climbing and become experts at it. They all love honey and are quick to ferret it out. They seem to know their tough hides are impervious to bee stings, and they are willing to sacrifice their noses for the goodies they seek.

Mother bear coddles and trains her young until that time when all black bears know they should release their offspring and let them earn their own way. We had the privilege of observing a mother bear and her two cubs romping in our campground. They climbed on our picnic table and upset the basket, clawing at items of interest and shredding others. Finally, the mother bear led her two darlings to a large pine tree, and with a few motherly grunts instructed them to climb up it and to climb up high. This they did, and mother ambled off, never to see them again. The cubs are given instructions to stay in the tree. This they do until a few days without food coaxes them down. By then mother is miles away and involved in a new life.

Animals are useful to man for meat, wool, silk, leather, fur, and dairy products. And of course we know how useful they are to pull heavy loads. Some serve a function that would be hard to fill in any other way. The camel, for instance, is irreplaceable for desert travel. On the whole, the most valuable animal is the one working in partnership with man.

We have not yet spoken about deer, beavers, badgers, raccoons, nor hundreds of other animals. The forests, fields, and mountain glades abound with wildlife. Much tender concern underlies the animal kingdom, as well as all of nature. We have seen how the loyalty of certain animals to each other, their love and faithfulness to the pattern of family life set for them by their Creator, can be an inspiration to us.

When nature is in balance, the animals' needs are amply provided by the Creator, as they live each day, moment by moment. Man would do well to consider deeply the wonder of God's care, which extends to man as well as animals. *How great are thy works, O Lord! Thy thoughts are very deep!* (Psalms 92:5)

Dogs

There is a favorite old hymn written by Cecil Alexander in the mid 1800s that begins: *All things bright and beautiful, All creatures great and small, All things wise and wonderful, The Lord God made them all.* It goes on to speak of each little flower, the bird that sings, sunsets and purple mountains, the running streams, the fruits of our gardens, and the little creatures so wonderfully made.

Dogs are such creatures. They are God's gift to man, and many stories have been told of the faithful friendship of dog to man and man to dog. Of all animals, perhaps dogs are the closest to man. Just why, we do not know, unless the utter devotion of a dog exemplifies for man an ideal of divine loyalty that reaches beyond reason and into the very heart of God.

Recently I witnessed such a fellowship. It was a beautiful day at the beach. People were leisurely strolling along, admiring the ocean as the tide dashed upon the smooth sandy beach. Out of the midst of the crowd came a man's cheery voice, commanding, "Get over on your own side of the sidewalk, Dodo! Don't be a hog. Remember, you're a dog. Freda, come along!"

A string of loud, jovial commands followed. I turned aside to see the populace give way to a man guiding two dogs on leashes, one, a very large, white Afghan, the other, a very tiny red dachshund. The three paused while tourists admired them and their owner shared tidbits of their exploits and amusing habits.

"Dodo, don't stand on Freda's foot. She's likely to bite you!" This was obviously meant as a joke, and the bystanders snickered as the white Afghan shifted his weight and smiled good-humoredly as Freda wiggled her long rope-like tail, looking up at him admiringly.

The man was somewhat of a showman and was having a great time with his companions. The crowd watched them as they coursed happily off down the street. They passed the corner, and the man's commands continued until they gradually faded into the distance. It had been a scene of agreeable comradeship, a man and his dogs.

The history of dogs goes back to European Middle Stone Age man who tamed wild dogs to help him hunt game. As time went on, the dog earned his way into man's heart and home. Today it would seem that almost everyone has either owned a dog at one time or has had contact with one.

The Bible contains over thirty references to dogs, many of which refer to masses of wild dogs that behaved unseemly. Because of this, the name *dog* became a word of reproach, the dog being considered unclean by the Hebrews. Although dogs are now held in fairly high regard by most people of the world, Moslems still do not like dogs, and Hindus in India try to avoid even touching a dog. This contrasts to some Chinese people who have been known to eat dog flesh for food.

It is interesting to note that as the primitive instincts of man evolve into more spiritual paths, the nature of love is exemplified increasingly in all that surrounds him. The spiritualization of the race has now produced new varieties of beauty, both in bloom and in beast. The quality of love intensifies.

Although dogs have submitted to the dominion of man, they retain many natural tendencies from ancient days, such as gobbling down their food lest an enemy approach from ambush and steal their food before they can eat it. At the first sign of danger, a dog will draw its tail between its legs lest it be damaged. He values his tail as well as his food and strives to protect both.

Have you ever wondered why a dog will turn around several times before lying down? This is a natural habit retained from long ago when dogs slept in open hay fields. They would move around in a circle to tramp down the long grass and make a soft bed to curl up on. Then, when they rested, the tall grasses left around them would hide them and give them camouflaged protection.

Every dog owner will tell you that his dog is the most intelligent of all animals. This may indeed be true of certain dogs, as there is a great variance in intelligence between individual dogs and the breeds of dogs, as well as how they are raised and trained. From many observations, the poodle appears very apt in taking instruction and is often used in circus performances, although sometimes a common mongrel seems to be exceptionally bright. Actually, we can never call anything ''common,'' because each creation is unique and special in its own way. *''What God has cleansed, you must not call common.''* (Acts 10:15)

Perhaps you own a dog that shows exceptional intelligence or bravery. Medals for bravery have been earned by thousands of dogs who never received them, nor were they even recognized for their deeds. I recall a dog who jumped into the river where we swam as children. It was a dangerous place near the falls, deep and wide, with a swift current. We were cautioned to stay away from the middle and remain near the shore. But this hot summer day, a strong man was daring the might of the current. As he swam brashly out into the middle of the stream, he was caught suddenly in the current and pulled under, just before the dam where the water was flowing over into falls on the other side.

Instinctively the dog knew his master was in trouble. While we children stood breathlessly on the riverbank, the dog leaped in and swam fearlessly out into the stream to save his master. The dog disappeared, then surfaced for a gasp of breath, then down he went again. There was a struggle as the man barely surfaced with the dog, only to disappear before our anxious eyes. Both dog and man drowned before a rescue team could arrive. Physical life had departed, but love lived on. I shall never forget the look of defiant loyalty in the dog's eyes as he leaped in to try to save his beloved master's life. He did not hesitate to consider how many harsh words or how many meals he had received or not received. He acted in love and faith. How much we can learn from a simple, faithful dog.

Many waters cannot quench love, neither can floods drown it. If a man offered for love all the

wealth of his house, it would be utterly scorned.
(Song of Sol. 8:7) *"I have loved you with an everlasting love; therefore I have continued my faithfulness to you."* (Jer. 31:3) So says the Lord.

Faithfulness and loyalty have eternal value that goes beyond human estimate. The union of man to his mate, children, household, community, state, and nation defies the enemy and confounds the destroyer. Loyalty is hidden in a Source higher than oneself and gives security and sure, eventual reward. Such reward may not be immediately forthcoming, nor may it return to us from the one we have loved. But love is of God, and faithfulness in love has a universal law that demands reward. So be patient and wait. For in due season your reward will be forthcoming. Nothing can stop it; it is God's decree.

On the lighter side, we once had a toy Boston terrier, Mitzi, who delighted in jumping into bed between my husband and me and pulling up the sheet around her neck with her teeth. There she would lie, head on pillow, eyes closed, as if to say, just ignore me, folks, I'll stay here for the night. Sometimes we would find her hiding under the bed to wait for the light to go out. You can probably tell of similar circumstances with your lovable pet!

We also had a beautiful water spaniel that our

150

girls named Patty. Mitzi and Patty played well together until we decided to take an extended trip and planned to leave them both at home. Our toy terrier was especially unhappy and continued to plead to go in every way she could think of. She even climbed into our suitcase after first casting out the clothes to make room for herself. When her anguish became so pronounced we could no longer ignore it, we yielded and told her she could go. The tiny animal was beside herself with joy! She raced down the stairs and out through the front door into the yard where Patty was idly standing. Mitzi raced up to Patty. They talked together in the way that dogs do, with their noses together. Immediately Patty's head drooped, her tail went between her legs, and she slunk to the shed, undeniably griev- ing. Mitzi was going on the trip, but she, Patty, had to stay home! Who said animals are dumb?

Some stories about dogs are almost unbelievable. Famous dog performers such as the wonder-dogs, Rin-Tin-Tin, Lassie, and Strongheart of movie fame prove that this creation of the Lord has been given great intelligence, as well as other endearing qualities too valuable to be casually overlooked.

There is a court record of a famous trial in the State of Missouri, where a speech by former senator, George G. Vest, won $150 in damages for his client. In 1870 that was an enormous sum of money. To quote a partial excerpt from his speech before the jury, which was considering the crime of a man who had killed his client's dog, he said: *The one absolutely unselfish friend that a man can have in this selfish world, the one that never deserts him, the one that never proves ungrateful or treacherous, is his dog.* He continued to say that a dog will remain faithful and true to one through poverty or prosperity, and that he will gladly sleep on the cold ground in the winter winds, only to be near his master. He will kiss the hand of his master when he has no food to offer, and he will seek him out when all other so-called friends have deserted him.

Such human friends come few and far between! And how precious is the friend who measures up. The best time to discover who your friends truly are is when you are dishonored, abused, or an outcast. (This test is not always possible.) However, *a friend in need is a friend indeed.* The friend *in deed* who comes to the aid of his companion in need is always remembered deeply and fondly over the years. One may relate this to the relationship of David and Jonathan. Even when David had to run for his life, due to the jealousy of King Saul, Jonathan remained a true friend and sent help to David time and again. Jonathan's lifelong loyalty to David and his untimely death were forever remembered by

David, who later sought out Jonathan's crippled son and helped him in every needed way.

A dog will humbly seek to earn his keep. He protects the home and barks when strangers threaten, even attacking, if necessary, to protect the loved ones inside. Monks of the hospice of Saint Bernard in the Swiss Alps trained their huge dogs to rescue travelers caught in the deep snow. The famous Saint Bernard, Barry, saved more than forty lives.

Dogs are useful in numberless ways. In Belgium they draw carts with heavy loads. In Germany boxers and Doberman pinschers accompany many a policeman on his lonely night beat. In the East dogs have been used for centuries to protect the flocks from wild animal attack. During World War II the United States Army trained dogs in the K-9 Corps to carry important messages and medical supplies to injured men on the battlefield. In Canada dogsleds are drawn by teams of huskies.

Every year in Laconia, New Hampshire, there is an international dogsled contest for beautifully trained huskies to show off their strength and cooperation. As groups of bystanders cheer, the teams pull out from the starting line at the village mall, each dog in its proper place, doing its share of the teamwork. Hours later the same teams pull past the finish line, hot, tired, foot-weary, each still drawing its share of the load and very conscious of the importance of teamwork.

These days much is said about team effort, and seemingly some dogs do better than some humans. However, we are observing improvement. The Bible says: *For everything there is a season, and a time for every matter under heaven.* (Eccles. 3:1) The time has now come for the world to change for the better. Men and women working in willing cooperation for the concern of many are expressing the activity of love. Couples, families, churches, morally-concerned social and political groups, God-directed governments—all are beginning to harmonize in a supreme effort to bring in a new heaven and a new Earth through the power and presence of God's Holy Spirit. And teamwork was an early American custom. As men banded together to help one another build homes, a town rose out of a forest. Working together, men and women created schools and churches. Being of one mind, the colonists cooperated and established a great nation known as the United States of America, united in thought, in devotion to God, and in deed.

Another type of teamwork is observed between blind people and their guide dogs, who guard and lead their unseeing masters and mistresses through dangerous city traffic, giving them opportunity to become useful individuals with intelligent occupations in the world. Helen Keller is one fine example of a blind person who has let her light shine in the hearts and minds of thousands who otherwise might have been helpless slaves of their infirmities.

The owners of purebred dogs are proud of their papers, but have you ever heard the owner of a mongrel boast? One sees some odd mixtures. One such was Jolly Boy, a mongrel we got in the Midwest while visiting there for a month. We called him Jolly Boy to perk up his spirits, because when he came to us he was the saddest-looking little shaggy dog one could ever imagine. He had the long, low body of a dachschund, a short, stubby tail, and a thick, gray, grizzled coat of a Scottie-spaniel mixture. He took a great shine to my husband, and the day before we were to leave town he quickly picked up the fact. (How do dogs know?) The next morning he arrived on our doorstep with five other strays. Every time we opened the car door or the tailgate of our ranch wagon to put in a box or suitcase, in would jump all five dogs! We finally sidetracked them by putting down bowls of dog food behind the house.

Scientists trying to uncover the source of intelligence examined a dog's brain and found that, compared with man's brain, a larger portion is devoted to smelling and hearing. They have also discovered how it is that a dog can be trained to be obedient, but they are still wondering how dogs are able to make the deductions they seemingly do. It seems logical that the animals' connection with the infinite mind of the Creator is an essential factor in their ability to draw certain conclusions and to respond discriminatingly. The stories of dogs who pick up a trail of a loved one long after hundreds of people have passed across it are astonishing. They appear to be guided not only by a highly-developed sense of smell but also by a mental connection with their loved ones and an inner guidance by their Creator.

One such story is told of a small mutt in the Midwest who was given to neighbors when the family moved to a large metropolis on the West Coast. The dog disappeared shortly after the family had left and hitchhiked to the family, limping into their yard months after they had become settled. When the story hit the radio, truck drivers recalled picking up a dog of that description limping along through the hot desert and toting it into Los Angeles. We can imagine the joy of the children as they embraced their faithful friend, and the gladness of the little dog reunited with its beloved ones! We might well ask, was this just a physical sense of smell that was a tool for reunion, or was there a faculty of love in operation about which man is still uninformed?

A dog's hearing catches high pitches far above the human range of hearing. Thus, when we blow the dog whistle for Fido, no one hears but Fido. We have learned that a dog's hearing is so sensitive that it can easily distinguish between musical notes, even though only a quarter tone apart.

Have you ever wondered why your dog pants on a hot day? This is because dogs do not perspire as human beings do. By panting, they cool off the inside of their bodies with the extra air they take in. They perspire through the soles of their paws, but this is a very small surface compared to the size of a dog's body. So we can see how important it is not to coop up our pet mercilessly in a box or hot car for long periods of time, but to allow it plenty of fresh air. A dog also needs plenty of cool drinking water on hot days, and water should always be available to him.

The plight of thousands of enslaved dogs being used for experimental purposes is being researched and brought to light. A few discoveries useful to humankind have resulted from these experiments, for example, the conditioned reflex and the action of insulin, but other, better means of research are being sought to eliminate this unnecessary cruelty and to release these tortured thousands from their cages. As man evolves in love and compassion, he detests to participate in such experiments.

Many feel that a dog does not have a soul, that when it is dead, it is dead and that is the end of it. Nevertheless, there are many dog owners who cherish the thought that someday their favorite pet will be reunited with them in some way and in some place. Certainly if the Lord of love made dogs to express love to mankind, He must in turn have a plan for the ongoing of this beautiful creation and its input into the soul of man.

Not long ago a picture was taken in Nashville, Tennessee, at Orleans Drive. In this photo is a graphic historical record of an unusual occurrence. It seems that a dog was struck and killed by a motorist in the early morning rush traffic. Three dogs kept vigil over their companion as its body rested on the sidewalk. Witnesses who observed the scene of the tragedy said the three original dogs were relived in shifts by six others, each taking turns as a circle of three in silent vigil. This continued for over two hours, until the body was removed from the sidewalk where it had been placed. What were the three dogs doing? Was their silent guard a sign of their sorrow? Were they watching something take place in the body of the one killed that humans could not see? Or were they praying in dog language, if indeed dogs have a language? We do not know. But the fact remains that the dignity, honor, and respect, as well as compassion, that were portrayed by these stray dogs far exceeded many human responses. How much we can learn from a dog!

Laughter mingles with tears as dog lovers recount stories of their favorite pets. I love to tell about Mr. Tuttle and Teddy. Every Friday Mr. Tuttle would chug up Mechanic Street in his old Ford truck with a camper on the back, not filled with people but with fresh fish. Teddy was our wirehaired terrier who loved Mr. Tuttle, mainly because after making a sale, Mr. Tuggle would carefully weigh up the purchase on his scale that dangled from the back of the truck and then throw Teddy the scraps. Teddy would stand by politely until the final act, namely, the fish scraps being thrown his way, and then with a lunge and a gulp he would devour his portion.

Teddy was somewhat of a vagabond. Every day he would trot off to town and make his rounds, greeting his doggie friends along the way. Everyone in town knew Teddy. And because Mr. Tuttle knew Teddy, often Teddy would bum a ride home with him, up the mile-long road to our house in the country.

On a hot summer day, Teddy came across Mr. Tuttle at the beginning of Mechanic Street, and Mr. Tuttle obligingly asked Teddy if he wanted a ride home. Teddy quickly hopped up on the front seat and proudly rode along, looking straight ahead as he passed his pals along the way.

At one house, a lady gave Mr. Tuttle a piece of cake which he could not eat at the time, so he put it on the seat between him and Teddy. The dog took no apparent notice as they rode along together. The last house came in view, and Mr. Tuttle stopped to make a sale. When he returned to the wheel, Teddy was still staring straight ahead, not moving a whisker. The cake was gone.

Teddy was a very loyal dog and lived to a ripe old age of 70, if one counts dog age as seven years to one. He had many pals in the neighborhood and carried on a running competition with Fritz, a mongrel German shepherd who lived next door. Never did Teddy ride by in our car but that he stuck his head out the window and barked, to let Fritz know he had the upper hand.

Fritz was owned by a young couple and their three children and was greatly beloved by all the family. When the father lost his job in the local hat factory, the family decided to move to the city where another job was offered him. In the process of moving, Fritz was given to the neighbor up the street. The family hated to give him away, but they could not take him to their apartment in the city.

The family left, and Fritz's new owner tied him securely. But Fritz chewed his rope in half and was soon back at the empty house, rope dangling, looking forlornly for his family. Where had they gone? How could they leave him behind? Didn't they know he was part of their family?

Time and again the dog broke his rope. Then a chain. Each visit was more pathetic as the dog became obsessed with finding his family. His anguish was expressed by loud yelps of grief as he ran around the house, looking for a way to get in to search for his family.

Time and again the new owner came and took him home, until Fritz finally realized he had been left behind for good. The pathos of such a situation is frequent when we, in our fluid state, leave our pets behind. Many pets are not so fortunate as Fritz but are dumped by the roadside to starve or get run over. Has not our Creator given us these beloved pets to teach us valuable lessons of caring? When will we learn them? Many poets have caught glimpses of what may go on in a dog's mind when faithfulness and love have become a one-way relationship. Fritz gradually accepted his new master, much to the relief of his neighbors.

We are coming into a new era where man and his world will praise the Creator, for he will find himself at peace through his Christed bond of oneness with all life. *Praise the Lord! . . . Let them praise the name of the Lord! For he commanded and they were created.* (Psalms 148:1, 5)

Butterflies

m. Russell
AGERONIA Hubner, butterfly

This is the age of butterflies! Not only do we have the most beautiful of all creatures fluttering over our flower beds, we have many varieties of "human butterflies" fluttering from one organization to another, one religion to another, one community to another, one country to another. Trailers and mobile homes roll, planes wing their way to remote corners of the Earth. People hike and bike with knapsacks, they tour with tents, and they busily communicate with each other, exchanging bits of information.

This extension of human effort is part of our search for understanding. In this search, like a butterfly that occasionally visits the "wrong" flower, we disengage ourselves from paths that do not work and move on and up. There is an inner guide that whispers, "Try again; don't give up; keep on the upward wind,'' and with that, progress is made.

Butterflies are creatures of the light. They float from flower to flower gathering the sweets free for the taking, basking in the warm sunshine, quivering with delight.

We are also creatures of light. We secretly know our identity reaches far beyond the dense, finite form we now manifest and that our conscious destiny someday will be in the light. Even now we are one with the light, but we are just beginning to see it. A few forerunners of the race have been illumined, and they report the glory of the light, so we know it exists. We pray, "Open my eyes, Lord, that I, too, may see!"

How is this light dawning in awareness today? Through the mental level of our experience we are learning how to attune more perfectly to Spirit and how to harmonize our emotional nature to it. True, some of the avenues of our search are fraught with hazard, but there is an inner drive that carries us on to better ways, and God is not a judge of action but of inner attitude. Is ours the urge for self-gratification or for Self-glorification?

Have you ever watched a butterfly dip into a flower head and then flit off to another? It samples the wares of many in the course of a day. People grow in awareness in similar fashion. They dip into deep philosophical discussions, meditation, prayer

experiments, metaphysics, biofeedback, psycho-
therapy, hypnosis, astrology and so on. Parapsy-
chology is taking new twists and turns, as scientific
experiments delve into the field of extrasensory
perception. As we probe the powers of mind latent
within us, we are gradually led in awesome wonder-
ment to the great universal Mind wherein lies the
fount of all wisdom and knowledge.

In watching a butterfly hatch out of a chrysalis
you have no doubt been amazed to see the rapidity
with which it develops. From a wrinkled, paper-
thin roll, the lovely wings evolve. The creature
slowly stretches and spreads itself on a hospitable
leaf or lawn. Little by little the ends of the tail
develop until the whole design is complete. Each
species of butterfly has its own design as distinctive
as a company seal or a family coat of arms. By its
color and design you can identify any butterfly you
may be looking at and know which one of the 700
kinds it may be.

The life cycle of a butterfly is interesting. Beginning as an egg laid separately, or in a cluster on a
juicy leaf by its mother, the creature hatches into a
worm known as a caterpillar. As soon as this happens, the creature begins its devouring process as it
hungrily consumes the foliage around it. The cabbage butterfly is a good example of the damage
that can be done by a hungry caterpillar. However,

butterfly caterpillars in no way equal the damage of that done by night-flying moths. Their harm is minor in comparison to the beauty and usefulness they contribute to life.

Very frequently the larva state, or caterpillar, is adorned with hairs, spikes, and tubercles of various forms. The body is jointed, usually consisting of thirteen rings or segments with a head and anterior segments that will become the legs of the butterfly when it is fully developed.

The middle of the body is built for locomotion, and the caterpillar has good equipment for eating which differs profoundly from that of the butterfly. Whereas the butterfly's tongue is made to suck liquids, the caterpillar is equipped with sharp, cutting mandibles that can shear off tiny strips of leaves it feeds upon. If you have ever observed a caterpillar at lunchtime you will notice it holding the leaf in place with its three pairs of legs, so it can get plenty of nourishment in a hurry.

The greedy creature soon becomes quite fat and uncomfortable in the skin in which it was born, and a molting process takes place as the creature splits the skin along its back and crawls out of it. Before this happens, however, it has had presence of mind to attach its skin to a leaf or branch to which it will remain attached during the chrysalis state.

The Creator has provided intricately for every comfort and necessity for the complete and final production of a butterfly. It is amazing to see the delicate thought that has gone into such a humble creature as a worm. The caterpillar is able to spin silk from a viscous fluid secreted from sacs located in the dorsal region, under the head, just back of the mandibles. The fluid silk is squirted out through an elongated tube. With this the creature is able to do all kinds of wonderful things!

The caterpillar can use its silken thread to lay down a path from one leaf to another, one branch to another, or one tree to another; and then, like the story of Hansel and Gretel, follow its thread safely back to its original home. Unlike Hansel's bread, no other creature desires to eat the silken thread, so it remains safely in order.

Another use, besides attaching its skin to the leaf or branch, is to tie together the leaves that will become its chrysalis. The silk is also used to make the little buttons and girdles by which the chrysalis is fastened together and held in place. The old song, "Button Up Your Overcoat" applies to the caterpillar as it prepares for the period of time when it reaches the pupal stage. Its little girdle of silk is spun around it and the leaf that is to become its chrysalis, much as an Indian baby is strapped to its mother's back.

What takes place in the body of a caterpillar as it molts and retreats inside its little house is quite mysterious. The Bible tells us that God chooses the simple things of the world to confound the wise, and surely this is true in this case. The transformation of a worm into a glorious butterfly is nothing short of a miracle!

If one were to cut open a chrysalis, one would discover the complete makings of a mature butterfly—the body segments, sheathing plates, the wings, and all the other organs necessary for the life of a butterfly. What wisdom is involved in the simple life of a butterfly!

A joke is often told about two caterpillars watching a butterfly overhead and one worm bragging to the other, "You'll never get *me* up in one of those crates!" If we were to compare our lives to the life of a butterfly, doubtless we could look back and see our spiritual, mental, and emotional progress. You surely are thinking, believing, and doing things today you never thought *you* would do!

As humanity proceeds from the baby stage of God's loving care, it develops into a defined pattern for existence, growing in awareness of a higher power, until the day when it will finally take wing and be carried by the wind of the Holy Spirit to new dimensions of life heretofore unknown to us.

Chrysalids vary in shape and in color, as well as

the length of hybernating time, until the beautiful creature emerges. Some remain in the chrysalis stage for only a few days or weeks, while others pass the winter in that state. The latter is true of butterflies in the northern climates.

If you have an opportunity, it is well worth the time and effort to remain quiet and watch the panorama of a butterfly emerging from its chrysalis. The transformation is quite remarkable. The creature splits its coverings, throwing its head, legs, and antennae forth and proceeds to draw its long worm-like mass out of its former sheathings. In a solitary position, with head upward and its long body downward, the creature's heart pumps nourishment into the body, which responds rapidly to the circulation, particularly in the wing section.

As you watch, wings will take form before your eyes. Moment by moment they grow and develop into beautiful wings with perfect markings that identically correspond to their species. This has all been carefully plotted and planned by the masterminded Creator, and the creature is simply responding to the Creator that whispers by an inner knowing: grow, grow, grow. This same whisper resides within you and me. Are we heeding it and obeying its impulse to become the beautiful children of God we are called to be?

Quietly the butterfly, now fully developed, rests

as its wings dry in the sun and the tiny scales and hairs feel for the first time the joy of expression. Then, very carefully the creature moves its wonderful wings. Shortly, it decides to try to fly. We cannot begin to imagine the experience of such an event! Off into the sunshine it flies, never again to return to its former life. It has been reborn, a new creature in Christ!

If you have ever caught a winged beauty you probably have noticed how a kind of dust sticks to your fingers. The dust is actually minute scales fastened to the membrane of the wing in such a wise fashion that no air may pass through. With some of these scales wiped off, the creature is maimed and unable to fly. The Latin name for butterfly is Lepidoptera, which actually means "scaly-winged." Blood circulates through these wings as well as through their well-developed brains.

With its tongue, called a proboscis, the butterfly sucks up nectar from flowers and drinks water occasionally. The knobbed antennae are used as feelers and serve as contact points with the outside world. Some butterflies, such as the red admiral or mourning cloak, have their noses on their feet, a comical turn of affairs.

A butterfly's eyes are multifaceted and gather light from all directions so that it can look up or down, forward or backward, as well as outward, all at the same time. Butterflies especially like the color red. A yellow swallowtail on a red bee balm flower is a sight to behold!

Butterflies are well-organized in their instinct to procreate and bless that part of the Earth to which the species is best suited. They often have an elaborate courtship and mating behavior. In a world of millions of insects one may wonder how the species remains pure, with only those of a kind mating. The good Lord of creation has provided an order even in this. On the hind wing there is a scent pocket from which both male and female spread their odor on their wings. This fragrance identifies the species. It varies with each family. A butterfly's sense of smell is accentuated during mating season, and like is attracted to like. A butterfly also uses its scent to drive away its enemies.

An observer has told us of watching a male grayling butterfly take up his position on the ground, waiting for a virgin female grayling to come along. She catches his fragrance and settles on the ground near him. He walks around and faces her, opens and closes his front wings, and shows off his beautiful pattern of colors. Then he seems to bow and approach her, embracing her antennae between his two front wings in quivering delight. He imbibes her fragrance, and she absorbs his. This gives the final stimulus for the male to unite with her, placing his sperm in the female's body where the eggs are retained until thoroughly water-proofed and ready to be deposited. In most cases the male signals and the female comes quickly to his call.

The observation and study of butterflies is very interesting. You may want to buy a book or butter-fly guide that will give you some valuable information on them. There will be some butterflies that you will like better than others. Some are rarer than others, some are quite common, although these lovely creatures are not as abundant as they used to be because of the increase in collectors.

Although the beautiful, large, orange Monarch is protected from predators because of its distasteful quality, it is still much sought after by those with nets. The lovely butterfly popularly called Diana has orange outer borders on the wings of the males, while the blue wing border is found on the female. This butterfly inhabits the southern Appalachian region and ranges as far south as northern Georgia and westward to Ohio and on to the Ozarks.

One butterfly is known for its pugnacious disposition. The Vanessa, found in southern California and northward up the coast into British Columbia, fights with the first butterfly that comes near it. Although it is pretty, it certainly does not strike a harmonious feeling with other butterflies that mildly share the nectar from a common garden spot.

Hunter's butterfly is found from Nova Scotia to Mexico and into Central America. It is a thing of beauty with its lively orange wings with brown stripes and large eye markings on the hind wings. It derives its name from the famous John Dunn Hunter who was captured by the Indians in his infancy and raised by them. He never knew who his parents were, but grew up like the Indians. Because of his outstanding ability to hunt game, the Indians called him "The Hunter."

After his first scalping expedition with the savages, he forsook them and went to Europe. There he amassed a fortune and became a friend of artists, adventurers, and men of letters. Because of his unusual background and his ability to share his former experiences, he became a sought-after favorite with the King of England and English nobility. The orange and red and blackish brown markings of this butterfly reminded the naturalist who named it of Indian war paint and, thus, the butterfly got its name.

In his book, "A Naturalist in the Amazons," Bates tells about a butterfly that makes a noise as it flies above the tropical forests. The insects make a clicking, grating sound, but no one has ever discovered how the noise is produced. It must be fairly loud to be heard above the sounds of a jungle.

Another popular butterfly is the large, Midwest tiger swallowtail. These lovely bird-like creatures have a wide-ranging genus and have been divided into many species for identification purposes. They are readily recognized by their large, paper-thin, yellow wings, with black tiger stripes and small but brilliant blue eye markings on the lower wing before the trailing tip fans out to give it its name, swallowtail. Men's formal wear is named from this creature because of the extended coat tails.

Butterflies, like humans, gather into crowds for mutual benefit. Some migrate each winter. When we hear of the Smiths and the Joneses who are traveling together with the Wilhelms in their campers from Maine to Florida, one might also think of the families of the painted lady or the red admiral that fly from California to Mexico for the winter months, or the millions of monarchs that travel together to the Gulf. Then again, perhaps you have seen, the next spring, a cloud of orange and black Monarchs in flight to cool Canada. Some butterflies fly across the Mediterranean Sea from North Africa to Europe to escape the summer heat.

As we think of the wonder of such delicate-winged creatures buffeting storms and wind, obeying that inner voice that directs their every move, we can learn a great deal. We, listening to the same voice of wisdom, are guarded and safely guided through the storms of mortal living.

The butterfly world is a world in itself and has its useful purposes that vary in degree and intensity far beyond our knowledge. Their beauty crowns nature with a liveliness quite rare. The wisdom that drives each to develop through its life-cycle in perfect order is in us all, should we as humans heed it. The provision of each organ for every function, from the silken thread of a cocoon to the brilliantly colored wing pattern, shows us the loving provision of a Creator who cares.

In his touching book, "I, Monty" Marcus Bach, illumines the thought that when a butterfly is in a certain stage of unfoldment, that is all he knows of himself. If he is an egg, that is his all. If he is a worm, to him that is the only world that could possibly exist. When he evolves further and forms a chrysalis, this again is the only life he views as probable. In a holographic sense this may be true—the part contains the whole, and the whole is in the part.

Until recently, mortal sense-man, like the butterfly, has been prone to question and discredit anything beyond his own immediate, limited scope of knowledge. But now as man matures, his horizon broadens. He can grasp a bit of the significance of being, and he is beginning to realize he is immortal, with unlimited potential. The adult butterfly is no longer confined within the walls of an egg, nor doomed to grovel in the earth as a worm, nor destined to the cloister. It is free, containing all this in its oneness with all life.

For thousands of years man was in the egg stage—that tiny seed containing the potential of God. He saw for a while only the walls of his ignorant thought accusing him. Then he developed, and even as a larva, he eked out his living from the herb of the field and the dust of the ground. Then the light broke forth. He looked up and contemplated that light, and he swayed back and forth on his safe little twig, thinking about life and light and his own self.

Stirring as a race, hoping, stretching in imagination, he was preparing for a day similar to when the butterfly spreads its wings on that first glorious morning of liberation and mounts in ecstasy to the sky. This is the day when man knows he has never been a captive of wall or twig or earth or sky, but of his own making.

The Creator has set before us, from the very beginning, an open invitation to *be* resurrected man, infinite being. It is as simple as that.

The Heavens

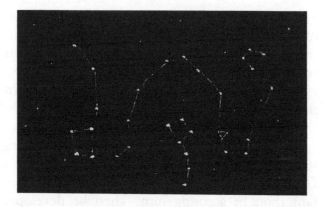

When I was young I used to kneel at my second-story open bedroom window and take deep breaths of the sweet night air. Somehow the night air always seemed to have a special essence. Later I learned there is more oxygen in the night air than in the daytime.

I also would look at the stars and try to count them. Soon the numbers would be forgotten as I became engrossed in the patterns that were apparent. Little by little I would find certain groups of stars and give them names. At that time I knew nothing about such things as constellations. And so it was that I called what is known as Orion's belt, "three sisters." Why not? Were they not all in a row and always in the same order? I often wonder how many other children go through this same stage of pondering, in a small way, the immensity and beauty of space.

Surely David considered such things in his heart as he watched his sheep on the beautiful starlit hillside of Bethlehem. After he became king, he had his chief musician bring his thoughts into focus with his psalm: *O Lord, our Lord, how majestic is thy name in all the earth! Thou whose glory above the heavens is chanted . . . When I look at thy heavens, the work of thy fingers, the moon and the stars which thou hast established; what is man that thou art mindful of him . . . .* (Psalms 8:1, 3, 4)

The freedom experienced by an astronomer must be greatly expanded as his mind reaches out into the universe while his body is confined to Earth. Perhaps this is an exercise we all should practice more often.

In the beginning, man must have watched the heavens with awe and wondered as the procession of stars, planets, and other points of light came into view. Perhaps he wondered if the stars were merely cracks in the heavenly fabric that stretched above his flat Earth, allowing heaven's light to shine through. Was there a great light behind the canvas that was showing through only at the worn spots? How far away was heaven? Were the lights he saw actual objects, fire objects, or what? Were they fixed or moving?

Somewhere around 600 B.C. the old myths of

dragons, demons, and gods in the sky began to be doubted. Two hundred years later Eudoxus decided that some were fixed, independent star bodies that appeared to move against a backdrop of more distant stars. Many conjectures were advanced which led to a more curious consideration of the Earth itself, which was believed to be flat.

Aristotle, the great Greek reasoner, observed that possibly the Earth might not be flat, but a sphere. He had no idea of its size, but later Eratosthenes calculated the circumference of the Earth, noting that the sun's rays fell vertically at noon in Syene (now Aswan, Egypt) at the summer solstice, while they fell at an angle of seven degrees at Alexandria, 500 miles northwest, at the same day and time. Eratosthenes correctly assumed that the sun was a great distance away, its rays practically parallel when they reach earth.

When he suggested that the Earth might actually rotate on its axis, he was laughed to scorn. They preferred their concept of a flat, motionless Earth, around which the whole universe rotated. It seems to be an altogether too human tendency to think we know it all. However, in these days, ego is being brought low before new illumined discoveries and insights.

Around A.D. 130, Claudius Ptolemaeus, known as Ptolemy, appeared upon the scene. He was a great thinker when it came to trying to make ordered sense out of the movements of planets and stars. He used intricate mathematical calculations to describe the motions of the planets and their relationship to one another, but he still supported the old concept that everything in the universe revolved around the Earth. After all, he reasoned, if the Earth moved or rotated, the birds would be swept away from their nests. This earth-centered view of the universe continued to be a firm belief in the western world for about fifteen more centuries.

By 45 B.C. the Roman calendar was ordered by Julius Caesar's decree to contain 365 days in a year, with one extra day every four years. In 1582 Pope Gregory XIII ordered that three leap years be skipped every 400 years to correct the falling behind of the seasons at the rate of one day every 125 years. The western world still uses the Gregorian calendar.

In the early 800s Arab scholars gathered at Baghdad and studied astronomy with many fine instruments made for measuring the positions of the stars and planets. With an instrument called an astrolabe, and a star map, they could sight stars and make careful astronomical calculations.

As we read about early explorers of the heavens, a Polish astronomer by the name of Copernicus elaborated on an old Greek idea of a planetary system with the sun at its center. He fortified his calculations with mathematical measurements but hesitated to publicize his findings. Finally, just a few hours before his death, he saw proof sheets of his book in its published form. Johannes Kepler and Tycho Brahe, working at the observatory near Prague in Czechoslovakia, continued to advance and elaborate on this idea. At Tycho's death, Kepler inherited his works and brought forth new laws which have been some of the richest discoveries in science.

About the same time, Galileo made a refracting telescope and made history with his published work, entitled "The Starry Messenger," in which he told of the distant objects he could see. We can imagine the excitement he must have created, and which must have stirred in Kepler himself, as he gazed through his homemade "spyglass" for a closer view of the moon and saw distant stars that humans had presumably never seen before. He proved that Venus shines from the reflected light of the sun, and observed the phases of Venus. He counted the four largest moons of Jupiter and looked at the moon's surface. A whole new world of wonder opened to him, and as a consequence opened to the rest of the world.

Now we know the sun is the center of our solar system, with nine planets revolving around it in their own ordered orbits. Mercury is the smallest planet in our solar system and the nearest to the sun. It is approximately one-and-a-half times the size of our moon.

Venus is the next closest to the sun and nearest in size to the Earth; it is therefore called the Earth's sister planet. At its brightest, it is brighter than any fixed star. We know it as the bright morning star and the brilliant evening star.

After Earth, whose one moon is about 238,000 miles away, there is the planet Mars, which has two moons. Mars turns on its axis and makes one complete revolution every twenty-four hours, thirty-seven minutes, and twenty-three seconds. A Martian day is a bit longer than an earthly day. The strange markings on Mars give rise to questions as to whether they are canals and if there is life on the planet, since it seems to have an atmosphere. Its summers and winters must be cooler than ours, since it is almost twice as far from the sun as is Earth.

A band of small heavenly bodies called asteroids lies between Mars and Jupiter. Jupiter is a very large planet, its size being over 1,300 times that of Earth. It has twelve known moons, and the planet is distinctive with its atmospheric bands that encircle it. A day on Jupiter is only some nine hours and fifty-five minutes long. You can imagine American businessmen trying to cope with such a schedule. A year, however, is almost like twelve years on Earth—plenty of time to get the tax returns in shape.

Saturn is about ten times larger than Earth, and it also has ten moons. Saturn is famous for its three wide rings composed of tiny satellites that swirl around the planet. It is believed that this planet must be very cold.

Uranus is about four times the size of Earth, and its year is equal to eighty-four earth years! In 1846, Neptune was discovered beyond Uranus, and Pluto was found in 1930.

Amazingly enough, it was not until the 1920s that scientists discovered our galaxy was one of billions. Up to that time man thought ours was the only galaxy in existence. Some scientists believe that our Milky Way galaxy is only one of many galaxies that circle a central sun, with other similar galaxies in outer space doing the same thing. Each is in its ordered path, and the glory of God continues to flow out in unending glorious expression. It was Tupper who said: *"Nature is the chart of God, mapping out all His attributes: art is the shadow of His wisdom, and copieth His resources."*

And speaking of order, did you know that there is a huge clock in the sky, which by our astronomical calculations, can tell us the seasons, the months, and the hours of the night? The center of its dial is the North Star.

You probably know which star is the North Star (Polaris), but in case you are not sure, there is an easy way to locate it. First, you need to find the Little Dipper (Ursa Minor). The dipper part of this starry constellation is comprised of four stars. Three more make up a handle. After you find it, simply line up the two stars at the end of the dipper and look out into space and find the first big star they point to. That is the North Star. The Big Dipper (Ursa Major) also has three stars in its handle and four stars in the dipper part.

The three stars in the handle of the Little Dipper serve as the hand of the clock. It swings slowly around the sky, suspended from its central hub, the North Star. Every twenty-four hours the hand makes one complete circle of the northern sky. Polaris has been the sailor's guide for thousands of years because it provides a stationary point of reference that is easily located. You can tell the months and seasons by the Big Dipper. On winter evenings, the Little Dipper is to the left of the Big Dipper, with its handle pointed up. The handle of the Big Dipper is pointing down. In summer, the positions are reversed. Because of the rotation of the Earth, the positions of the dippers change from evening to early morning.

The ancients, having little to do for long periods of time, amused themselves by weaving fantasies around the stars. In these days when we say the "Big M," we know that means hamburgers, shakes, and french fries. But the ancient Greeks, enamored by their imaginations, considered these five stars in the shape of an M to be a comfortable throne where queen Cassiopeia was seated. This queen was supposed to have been a beautiful queen of Ethiopia, but because of her attachment to extreme vanity, she was changed into a constellation.

An interesting parallel underlies this in that those who become vain over their personal appearance, or vain over personal success, often become crystallized into position and are unable to break loose from their own self-imposed mental confines. The biblical story of Lot's wife, who looked back, tells a similar tale of devotion to the physical aspects of life to such an extent that one is unable to break the spell and place one's full love and reliance on that power greater than oneself—God.

We are all familiar with ancient legends which personified the heavenly bodies. One of these, an old Blackfoot Indian legend of the creation, has been preserved in a mural in the Hayden Planetarium, which was painted by Charles Knight. The mural depicts the sun in pursuit of the moon, and to the left, seated on a high mountain under an arching rainbow, is The Old Man, Napi. Napi is the Indian's name for our Creator, who not only made the world but everything in it.

The earliest written record of this legend was found in an 1809 diary of Alexander Henry, a fur trader who roamed in all parts of the northern plains country and into Canada. According to his record, the Blackfoot believed that at first there was nothing but water, watched over by The Old Man, who had a female mate, but at that point no world children. The legend goes that eventually The Old Man divided the waters from the land and made the beasts, birds, fishes, and every other living creature. Later, a great flood came to destroy evil. When the waters covered the Earth there was only the tip of one mountain left where The Old Man sat, joined by four animals—the beaver, otter, duck, and muskrat. The muskrat dove down and brought some mud to the hand of the Creator, who reestablished the land.

The rainbow is spoken of by the Blackfoot as the Rain's Hat or The Old Man's Fish Line. It was therefore appropriate that Charles Knight paint a rainbow over The Old Man as he transformed the Earth after the cleansing flood.

What a change has taken place since ancient times. We have learned more in the last forty years about our solar system, it is estimated, than from all observations in the past. In early 1983 Earth's scientists looked at the evidence of planets beginning to arrange in ordered formation—creation itself was taking place under their gaze! The Infrared Astronomy Satellite (IRAS) sent twelve hours of data to Earth twice a day as a joint project shared by the United States, the Netherlands, and Great Britain. The Americans designed and built the 22.4-inch infrared telescope with its sixty-two detectors; the Dutch worked on the software and built the spacecraft systems; and the English controlled the spacecraft.

The satellite circled Earth in a 563-mile-high polar orbit and provided some exciting finds for astronomers. Awestruck scientists were not only able to observe firsthand what may be a new solar system taking formation, but have actually seen a number of stars in the process of being born! They were detected in dark clouds in the Milky Way galaxy. Unfortunately, IRAS has not worked since November 13, 1983, when it used up all its telescope coolant and could not "see" anymore.

The United States and other governments have also established research centers to investigate the claims of those who have allegedly seen unidentified flying objects. Thousands of such reports that have come from all over the world cannot be denied or ignored and have come under authorized investigation. There is an eagerness to discover intelligent forms of human life on other planetary systems beyond our own. Such enthusiasm has led NASA's Ames Research Center to search for radio signals that might come from intelligent extra-terrestrial civilizations.

The United States has also arranged to have our satellite telecommunications capable of being intercepted by other beings from outer space. A plaque attached to one of our space probe vehicles has the genetic code for human earth life, plus stick drawings of a man and woman on it, just in case someone from outer space wants to know.

Many surprises from these activities are being shared with the American public by scientists and astronomers. We now know that Jupiter also has a ring around it. Mars has many volcanoes. One, named Olympus Mons, is probably the largest volcano in the solar system.

Mercury has virtually no atmosphere. Venus has a heavy atmosphere of carbon dioxide and sulfuric acid, creating a greenhouse effect, with a surface heat of approximately 850°F. The photographs of the heavens, the planets, and especially of Saturn's rings (over a thousand contained in three large bands as seen from Voyager II) are so beautiful one wonders how our astronomers can contain all the beauty they are privileged to behold!

We understand that the NASA goal to produce a detailed infrared map of the entire sky may or may not be realized. We suspect that this may be only the beginning of a realization that they are touching the hem of infinity. In the book of Job, the Lord asked: *"Where were you when I laid the foundation of the earth? Tell me, if you have understanding. Who determined its measurements—surely you know! Or who stretched the line upon it? . . . when the morning stars sang together, and all the sons of God shouted for joy? . . . Can you lead forth the Mazzaroth in their season, or can you guide the Bear with its children? Do you know the ordinances of the heavens?"* (Job 38:4, 5, 7, 32, 33) It is our part, perhaps, to realize that the more we know, the less we know that we know.

Today we walk on the moon and launch space shuttles, and men who have actually stood on the moon and looked back over its lifeless rock piles to Earth have seen a glorious, shimmering blue-white planet—something to be treasured and something precious that needs to be preserved and needs to endure. Probably all the views man makes from outer space will eventually cause a response within the viewer to help him realize the prize we already own—a planet, fairest of all, of inestimable beauty, a gift from God.

Standing on Earth and looking toward the heavens, the most familiar and most easily discernable object we see is the sun. Of all the stars in the Milky Way galaxy, of which Earth is a part, our sun is the nearest star to Earth. The light from the sun makes life possible on Earth, and the heat produced by the sun comes from the burning materials in this star which are presumed to be hot gases. These gases come from chemical elements similar to those found in Earth, such as helium, hydrogen, calcium, sodium, magnesium, and iron. Our sun is like an atomic furnace, turning mass into energy. Every second it is estimated that it converts 657 million tons of hydrogen into 653 million tons of helium. The missing 4 million tons of mass are given to space in the form of energy.

The size of the sun is approximately 100 times the diameter of the Earth and approximately 400 times the diameter of the moon. Since light travels about 186,000 miles per second, it takes about eight-and-a-third minutes for the light from the sun to reach the Earth.

Our seasons unfold in natural order according to the relationship of the sun to the Earth. When, for instance, the sun is farthest from the equator in the northern hemisphere, we have the summer solstice, or the longest day of the year, which marks the beginning of summer. When the sun is farthest from the equator in the opposite direction, the northern hemisphere experiences the winter solstice, which is the shortest day of the year and marks the beginning of winter. Of course, we know that when the northern hemisphere has winter, the southern hemisphere is enjoying summer, and vice versa. When the sun's center crosses the equator and day and night are of equal length, we have the vernal equinox, which marks the beginning of spring, or the autmnal equinox, which marks the beginning of autumn.

It has been said that love is the power that holds the universe together. Perhaps it is that divine force behind the powerful gravitational pull of the sun on Earth and the other stellar attractions that is responsible for the law and order in our universe. We know that each body is necessary for the balance of the whole and that this balance is extremely delicate. When science tells us that a universal adjustment takes place when one as much as tosses a ball in the air, it makes one realize the significance of keeping Earth balanced by our obedience to God's laws.

As Earth turns, we become more and more aware of the complex envelope called atmosphere that envelops our planet, providing protecting layers against harmful radiations from the sun and allowing the sun's helpful rays to penetrate Earth. The atmosphere has four parts—the troposphere, stratosphere, ionosphere, and exosphere. The troposphere is that band of air that surrounds Earth up to a height of eleven miles at the equator and to a height of about five miles at the poles. This is the zone where our weather takes place. It is here that the glorious clouds form, raindrops assemble, lightning flashes, and rainbows arch the skies. It is here that dust particles and water prisms condense to produce beautiful sunsets.

As one ascends in the troposphere, the air becomes thinner and the temperature becomes colder. About five miles above the Earth is the jet stream, a belt around the middle latitudes. This phenomenon of an air current moving from west to east is used to great advantage by airplanes traveling in the same direction. Sometimes the jet stream goes as fast as 250 miles per hour. It is believed this stream may be the center of conflict between the polar cold and the tropical heat; therefore, it is neither permanent nor constant. Naturally it affects air travel, since this aerial escalator can speed up a plane in its flight or decrease it if it is moving from east to west.

Above the troposphere is the zone known as the stratosphere. Here the atmosphere is almost weatherless, it is crystal clear, and the cold temperature remains more or less constant. Air travel through the stratosphere can be very pleasant.

Above the stratosphere is the ionosphere. The air here is extremely thin, with scattered air particles that are electrified. Cosmic rays from outer space cause the ionization process. The highest layer of air is the exosphere. Ions of gas in the exosphere are very hot, reaching a temperature of 4,500°F. At night, the temperature of these particles drops to about -460°F.

Because we rely on oxygen to live, we cannot ascend very high into the thinning atmosphere of the troposphere without supplementing our oxygen intake. Mountain climbers may sometimes feel dizzy because they are not getting as much oxygen as they were accustomed to. Air is composed of two main gases, as you are no doubt aware: nitrogen and oxygen. Other gases, such as argon, carbon dioxide, hydrogen, ozone, and other more rare gases are also present.

The air also contains vapor and small amounts of solid matter, such as sea salt, dust and microbes, and pollen and spores from seed plants. Although the air is invisible, odorless, and tasteless, we know its presence by the stirring of the wind. Christina Rossetti once wrote a poem, ''Who Has Seen the Wind?'' and replied, *Neither I nor you: but when*

*the leaves hang trembling the wind is passing
through.*

In regard to our use of air, it is interesting to note
the airways or routes which are followed by airplanes. Often you can pick up a brochure on a
plane showing the various routes of that particular
airline as it follows a government-regulated net-
work. This was first developed in the United States
by the Post Office department to speed up airmail
deliveries. Now air traffic control centers have a
demanding job of preventing collisions as more
and more planes take to the air.

Many amusing stories are told of early air travel.
One of the most humorous may be that of Presi-
dent Teddy Roosevelt, who was invited to take a
plane ride with Arch Hoxsey in St. Louis, Missouri,
in 1910. This was in the days when planes resembled crates in the sky and were quite open to the
breezes. Waving to the crowds below, Mr.
Roosevelt almost fell out!

After flying to many lands throughout the
world, under many differing conditions, I was
amazed when I was told that the wing of a high-
speed plane must be so strong that four elephants
could stand on it without damaging the wing. The
average traveler has but little comprehension of the
physical laws that must be complied with in order
to master the air.

Regarding air rights, no one can own the air itself, but space above a parcel of land can be rented and built upon. The Chicago Merchandise Mart was one such building made possible by leasing of air rights. It stands over the right-of-way of the Chicago and North Western Railway.

For thousands of years, man had no idea of what made the weather or what controlled it. Because of this ignorance, great superstition surrounded it, and ancient priests innovated chants and dances to bring the rain to their parched ground, inviting unknown entities to favor them. But we can praise God that we are arriving at the age of enlightenment, at least so far as better understanding the reason for certain cloud formations and the formation of storms. We are beginning to learn how to control the weather and even bring rain if necessary.

Action in weather does not just happen; it is caused by heat or cold, moisture or dryness, and their interaction. Warm air always rises, as part of the built-in system the Lord thought of when He created this beautiful Earth. Air heats more quickly over land than over water. As the warm air rises, it is replaced by cooler air, pressure builds up, and the air moves in circulatory motion. Both man and beast profit by this principle of air pressure. The squid, scallop, and dragonfly nymph are jet-propelled, birds sail and soar, seeds are airborne on umbrellas, streamers, and silken balls. Animals are warmed or chilled, and even insects respond to the variations in weather.

As the sun heats the water, it evaporates and forms moisture which rises to produce the substance for clouds. Moist air is lighter because the mixture of molecules is different from that of dry air. The rising moisture can form clouds, to bring a variety of weather patterns.

Every cloud has a name. Four types of clouds we often notice when we look skyward are cumulus, cirrus, stratus, and nimbus.

The first type of cloud is the cumulus—those round, billowy masses that pile up and up in serene splendor. The word cumulus in Latin means "heap," which well describes these masses of billowy cotton as they float a mile or so high, laying pleasant shadows on the land beneath.

Cirrus clouds are those light, wispy ringlets, high above the other clouds, holding tiny ice crystals. You can see these lovely wisps dreamily off in the bright blue yonder, some five or ten miles high.

Stratus is a word that means "spread out." These are level strips of clouds often near the Earth, lying close to the horizon.

Nimbus are dark gray clouds loaded with rain. They are usually shapeless, hodgepodge formations with dark, threatening lower halves. Out of these proceed great quantities of water, sometimes cloudbursts, thunder, and lightning.

Job observed the thunder and lightning and wrote of it thus: *"Hearken to the thunder of his voice and the rumbling that comes from his mouth. Under the whole heaven he lets it go, and his lightning to the corners of the earth. After it his voice roars; he thunders with his majestic voice. . . . "* (Job 37:2-4)

Once opposite signs of electric charges are present in different layers of clouds, the stage is set for a discharge, either from within a cloud or from cloud to Earth. Some strange occurrences have taken place when lightning has struck on Earth. A recent discharge not far from my home is typical, however, of the destruction that may be wrought in nature, although it is surprising how seldom lightning strikes anything. During a thunderstorm, a bolt of lightning hit a tree, making a round hole about the size of a quarter, leaped down the trunk and burst forth about ten feet below, splintering the tree into a mass of pieces from that point to the ground.

Weather is often monitored by the use of balloons containing minute, automatic meteorological stations. These ballons are released daily at 0 and 12 o'clock GMT (Greenwich mean time). The balloon stops when it reaches the stratosphere, the level varying from day to day around the globe, for clouds are not found beyond the troposphere.

There are also whirlwinds born at sea that move in to land. There are waterspouts that draw water up into high columns under great pressure and speed. There are hurricanes, with whirling cones of whistling air, rain, and lightning. The center of the cone is calm and is called the eye. One type of hurricane is called a typhoon in the North Pacific Ocean. Typhoons are more quickly spent than hurricanes, being about a week in duration, whereas a hurricane can last several weeks and have a wider path of damage.

My late husband's father was sent to the Philippines as a missionary. During his sixteen years there, he translated the Bible into a native language and became interested in the Chinese culture. On their way home, the family decided to visit China. This they did, to their great danger. A typhoon struck the boat and dashed it onto the rocks. When the ship sent out signals of distress in the midst of the storm and heavy seas, a freighter heard their call and was soon there. As the ship was slowly sinking, an effort was made to get as many people off the fated vessel as quickly as possible.

My husband, then a child of seven, waited for the boat to tip, and at the right moment leaped from one ship to the other and was safely taken to shore. Although this may seem like a brave and dramatic thing for someone to do, I suppose that in the fury of the storm everyone's attention was so otherwise engrossed, it was treated as a minor occurrence. A storm of that ferocity is frightening, and much prayer is needed to maintain one's faith.

Another dangerous cloud formation is a tornado, sometimes called a twister. It is a funnel formation that causes violent destruction. I recall one time when two tornadoes were heading toward my home. One tornado was coming from the southwest, and the other was coming from the southeast. They were destined to meet over my home. A group of friends and neighbors were present, and while I took a few of those who wanted to pray inside the house with me, the others watched the sky scene with grave concern. They knew what would happen if the two met and touched down. As we prayed inside, the outside spectators saw the two tornadoes converge, go up into the heavens, and dissolve. All glory to our wonderful God!

Do you remember the story of the disciples in a boat on the water with Jesus asleep in the bow? Do you remember how the storm arose and the wind blew and the waves were so severe that the boat was sinking? They called to Jesus and woke Him. Do you recall what He said to them? *"Why are you afraid, O men of little faith?''* (Matt. 8:26) Perhaps the most important thing for us to remember is not the power of the storm or the extent of possible damage, but that we have been instructed to subdue the Earth and to have dominion over it.

As we unite our minds and hearts with God's holy will, our world and our weather will correspond with gentle days and loveliness in pleasantness, even as it was meant to be from the very beginning. *"For God so loved the world that he gave his only Son, that whoever believes in him should not perish but have eternal life."* (John 3:16)

On a very bright moonlit night sometimes the clouds are visible. Edward Rickenbacker's book, ''Rickenbacker,'' tells about his experience of being set adrift in the vast Pacific, no doubt you recall his report of the beautiful cloud formations he observed both day and night. Whether or not it was his imagination or a form of mirage is not clear, but he reported seeing pictures of cities, people, animals, birds, and various other scenes in the clouds.

Because there is an urge within us to seek and discover eternal truths, we continue to search and discover new things daily. As we study the weather, we find new ways of controlling it. As we observe the heavens, we find new pathways in the stars and new bodies of light that take on new meaning.

For some years Earth's satellite named Explorer

42 has been receiving from the deep recesses of space mysterious signals which travel at the speed of light. These signals apparently come from a source in our galaxy that is thousands of billions of miles away from us. Although the area of this source is smaller than that of Earth, its energy is at least four times more powerful than our sun. The strange situation is that it can double its energy output within a tenth of a second, but just as suddenly diminish its energy. The scientists have named this strange phenomenon Cygnus X-1.

It almost seems that as soon as man concludes that God's plan for the universe has gone astray and is about to fall apart, some new discovery appears to prove the universe is still very much in the control of the One who created it. The more we discover the wisdom underlying all creation, the more we proclaim, "How truly great Thou art!"

As we consider the magnitude of the Creator's infinite planning so as to contain and sustain and govern the universe, we become humble indeed. Order, peace, beauty, and majesty unfold as a panorama in sky and Earth and bring enduring blessings to us.

The heavens are telling the glory of God; and the firmament proclaims his handiwork. (Psalms 19:1)

Living Together

All Islands Join the Mainland

A friendly God pervades all nature and indwells humankind. Yet loneliness, it has been said, is much like the common cold. Most people are susceptible to it from time to time, some more so than others. Being lonely, however, has nothing to do with being alone. Our cities and towns are crowded with human beings very much with other people, but nevertheless lonely and insecure.

Loneliness is an individual experience that seems unrelated to an outer cause, the underlying reason being that one needs to realize the oneness of all living creatures, great or small, important or unimportant, rich or poor, favored or unfavored, gifted or poverty-stricken. In the understanding of life there is a uniting force that rests within us all and makes us all one, regardless of how superior or how distant we may think ourselves to be.

If you happen to be such a person, remember that all islands have mainlands and are in some way joined to them. All life is one, and therefore, what you are you can find in another. Notice one of your own traits or habits in another, relate to it, and experience that other person. Then the differences will become interesting and worthy of exploration.

Relating to life may seem to present a challenge. However, as you become interested in natural, growing, living things and observe the presence of divine love tending its own, you will feel loneliness sinking into the past and a new zeal for life replacing it.

There is nothing more interesting or exciting than life! It was Henri-Louis Bergson who said: *Life is increasing creation.* Those who attempt to follow the successive aspects of nature become lost in infinity; dullness and boredom cease.

The great thinker, John Dewey, urged us to realize that change is life and life is change, always bettering itself. Bergson agreed, remarking: *The course of change seems prepared at the instant of birth, even before birth.* It is almost as though *an accumulative memory of the past made it impossible to go back again.*

The great plan unfolds as a grand drama day

after day. Within the ceaseless change of life an ordered sequence rests securely and is obeyed by the smallest of creatures to the greatest.

The Creator has a plan for every living creature, and He has a plan for you. As you become thoughtful and search that inner kingdom, all will be revealed. Our marvelous Creator is patient, kind, and true in His response to all forms of life. He is much like a watchful, persevering parent, showering gifts upon us and observing our reactions. We are surrounded with such abundance of beauty and natural wealth it is past time we realized it.

Nature has placed its signs of patience and excellence, order and interrelatedness for us to read. Nothing is alone; all share a common life and are equal in opportunity to enjoy it. Rejoice, for the day is fresh and new! Look around you, O pilgrim, and behold the gifts of God. They are yours for the taking!

About the Author

Marjorie H. Russell is the founder of Arcadia School of Light, in Franklin, New Hampshire, a school helping people reach spiritual understanding and illumination through Bible study. She was ordained a Unity minister in 1961, and spent several years serving Unity churches in the New England area. Marjorie has also worked in the Silent Unity prayer ministry at Unity Village, Missouri, and has written several articles for *Unity* Magazine and *Daily Word*.

An international speaker, Marjorie's series of lectures on nature have met with a popular response. She has appeared on television and radio shows throughout the United States.

Marjorie was raised in Massachusetts, with, as she says, "the influence of Longfellow, Thoreau, Alcott, and Emerson." She has been a nature lover since childhood. "After-school time, weekends, and summers were spent outdoors, studying nature firsthand," she says.

Marjorie's late husband was a prominent educator. She has two children and six grandchildren.

Printed U.S.A.
171-F-7105-10M-9-84